JANE
GREENOFF

At home with

CROSS
STITCH

JANE GREENOFF

At home with

CROSS STITCH

David & Charles

Dedication
To my husband, Bill,
the wind beneath my wings

Music Sampler

A DAVID & CHARLES BOOK
Copyright text, designs and charts © Jane Greenoff 1994
Photographs © David & Charles 1994
First Published 1994

Photography by Di Lewis

Jane Greenoff has asserted her right to be identified
as author of this work in accordance with the
Copyright, Designs and Patents Act 1988.

A catalogue record for this book is available from the British Library.

ISBN 0 7153 0079 2

Typeset by BLANC VERSO
and printed in Italy by Lego SpA
for David & Charles
Brunel House Newton Abbot Devon

CONTENTS

INTRODUCTION

Looking back, this book always seems to have been inevitable, as it is a combination of the two all-consuming interests that keep me and my family, literally, in business. When I am not stitching or designing cross stitch, I love poring over glossy magazines and 'coffee-table' books to borrow ideas for our adored Cotswold cottage. Searching for 'props' for the photography for a book like this is the perfect excuse for filling my cupboards and dressers with china, glass and other useful bric-a-brac.

My husband, Bill, and I have worked together from home for three years, so we are acutely aware of how important a sympathetic home, and therefore work, environment is for the mind and body. As a dear friend quoted to me on her last visit: 'If you have enough money to buy two loaves, buy one and spend the rest on hyacinths to feed your soul.'

I love our cottage, as I loved the little semi-detached house that preceded it, and I enjoy collecting 'junk' (my husband's word) and stitching cross stitch projects for every room. The ideas for my designs come from all over the place. I carry my scribble book *everywhere* with me, as ideas for designs or projects will appear at any time, especially when peeling potatoes!

Sometimes the ideas come from my children. Living in the country is wonderful for them, but having grandparents who live at the seaside, they are both enchanted by the sea and anything and everything that can be collected from the shore. They decided that a seaside bathroom was the answer, and you can see the results on pages 66–73.

The projects in this book have been designed for the beginner and expert alike. Almost all the designs can be stitched in linen or Aida fabric so that stitchers of all levels should find ideas and projects that appeal to them. Where the design is most suited to linen I have indicated this in the text.

If you would like to reproduce the projects exactly as they appear in the photographs, you will need to select DMC stranded cottons. I have indicated an alternative Anchor shade number on all the colour charts, but a perfect match is not always possible. Some of the worked examples in the photographs require unusual fabrics and these should be available from good needlework shops, but in case of difficulty, you can obtain them by mail order (see Suppliers). In all cases it is possible to choose other fabrics and even dye them at home yourself.

The chapters in this book are based on rooms in an imaginary house, beginning with 'Sweet Pea Welcome' in the hallway. Many of the designs can be mixed and matched to make other projects and in some cases these are suggested in the text.

The designs in the photographs can be adapted and will suit both modern and traditional homes. Suggestions for framing and making up the projects are indicated in the appropriate chapter and in the section on this subject in Materials and General Techniques at the back of the book.

The dimensions given for each project are for the examples in the colour photographs. If you select alternative fabrics the corresponding design size will also vary, so you need to check the stitch counts for each project *before* you start stitching.

Some of the designs can be worked straight from the charts, but others will need planning before you begin stitching. Please refer to the section on planning in Materials and General Techniques.

If you intend to make a project for a book, a bag or something similar, you should refer to the making up section in Materials and General Techniques for guidance.

All dimensions shown are imperial with metric equivalents indicated in brackets.

I hope you enjoy selecting and stitching the projects in this book as much as I have relished designing and making them.

Happy stitching !

Four Seasons Clock

1

THE HALLWAY

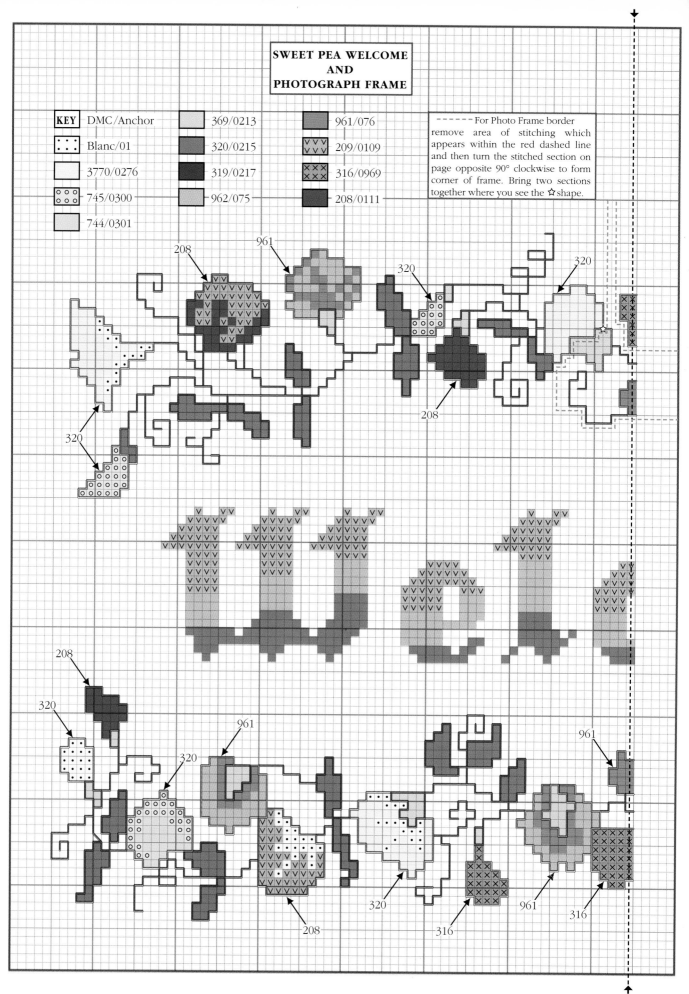

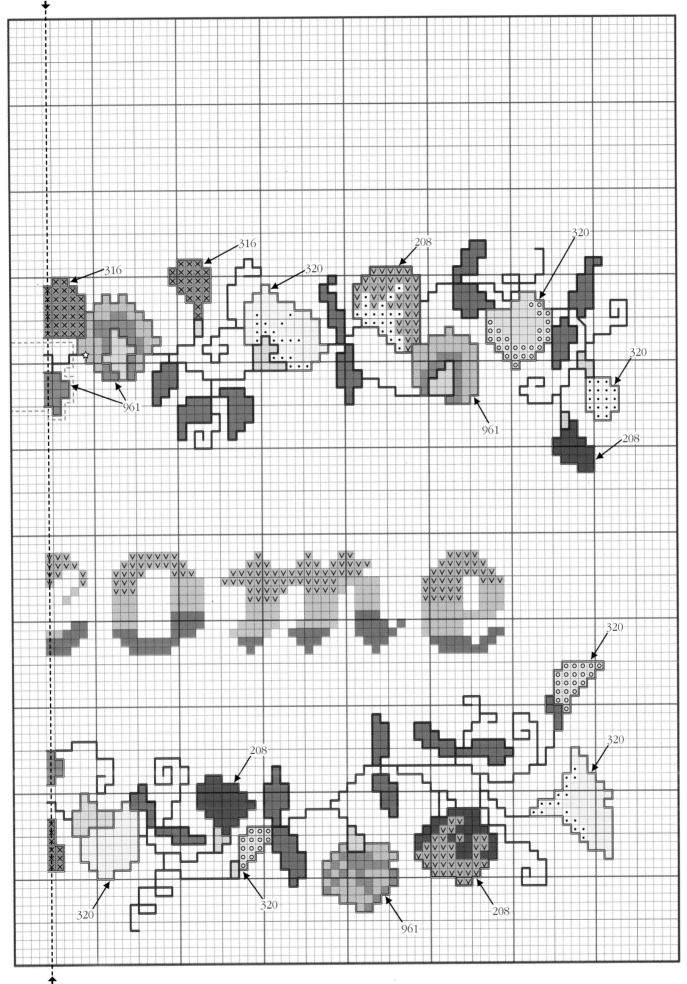

THE
HALLWAY

*Whatever the weather in the street outside, the entrance to a home should feel warm
and inviting (see pages 8-9). In my mind I have a picture of flagstone floors, an
umbrella stand and a faint scent of wood polish. In reality, our tiny porch is littered
with Wellington boots and Lego and the most likely smell is of drying waxed jackets!*

SWEET PEA WELCOME

Design size: 9½ x 5½inches (24 x 14cm)
Stitch count: 139 x 82

13½ x 9inches (34 x 23cm) antique lavender linen, 28 threads per inch (2.5cm)
Stranded cottons (floss) as listed on the chart on pages 10-11

1 Sew a narrow hem around the linen to prevent fraying.
Fold the fabric in four, press lightly and, using large tacking

(basting) stitches, mark the folds (see page 125).
2 Work the design from the chart on page 10, using strands of stranded cotton (floss) for the cross stitch one strand for the back stitch outline. The outline sha are shown on the chart.
3 When the cross stitch and back stitch are complete, chec for missed stitches, then press lightly on the wrong side before stretching and framing (see Materials and General Techniques, pages128-9).

SWEET PEA PHOTOGRAPH FRAME

This pretty photo frame (pages 8-9) has been stitched using the border from the Sweet Pea Welcome chart on pages 10-11. The design is stitched on stitching paper and mounted on self-adhesive mount board (see Materials and General Techniques, and Suppliers). If you are not familiar with stitching paper please refer to page 122 before starting this project.

1 To make the frame, select your photograph and measure the required aperture size. This can be lightly drawn on the stitching paper with a soft pencil.
2 The sweet pea border is worked from the chart on page 10,

turning the design where indicated. It might be helpful to draw the sweet pea pattern on some squared paper before you begin stitching.
3 Work the cross stitch from the chart, using three strands of stranded cotton (floss) for the cross stitch and two strands for the back stitch outline.
4 When the stitching is complete, protect the underneath surface and then cut the opening in the paper with a sharp craft knife. If using self-adhesive mount board, follow the manufacturer's instructions and frame as desired.

PANSY PICTURE FRAME

This lovely photograph of my paternal grandparents (pages 8-9) is framed in stitching paper with the simple corner motif from the chart on page 14 and the pansy adapted from the spring section of the Four Seasons Clock on page 15.

I used DMC stranded cottons (floss) 340, 554, 552, 310 and 743 to simplify the style of the flower, then added greenery to frame the petals. To make your own frame, follow the instructions for the Sweet Pea Photograph Frame.

FOUR SEASONS CLOCK

This lovely Four Seasons Clock (page 6) is not recommended for the complete beginner because the position of the design on the clock face requires planning. All the elements of the design are included in the charts on pages 14 and 15.

The clock in the colour photograph is a simple square design incorporating a quartz clock movement within a purchased picture frame. The sizes and materials given here are for the example in the picture. If you choose to use a purchased clock kit, you will need to adapt the design to fit your clock face.

Finished clock size: 14inches (35.5cm) square
Design size: 12inches (30.5cm) square
Stitch count: 168 x 168

17 x 17inches (43 x 43cm) jade green linen, 28 threads per inch (2.5cm) as listed
Stranded cottons (floss) as listed on the charts on pages 14-15
One pair of clock hands and one quartz movement

1 Sew a narrow hem around the edge of the linen to prevent fraying. Fold in four and mark the fold lines with a line of tacking (basting) stitches. Set aside while you plan the clock face.

2 Refer to Planning your Own Designs on page 128 and proceed as follows. Draw a square pencil outline on the graph paper to illustrate the outer limit of the design. Check the stitch count for the particular clock and fabric that you have chosen. Mark the centre of the clock face to position the spindle and hands. Using the charts on pages 14 and 15, draw the clock numerals in position and add the outline of the floral motif.

3 The design illustrated in the colour picture was stitched using two strands of stranded cotton (floss) for the cross stitch and one strand for all the back stitch outline.

4 The brambles in the bottom left section (autumn) were outlined as indicated on the chart and then completed with random tweeded French knots (see page 126) in a mixture of DMC 823, 522 and 601.

5 The star shapes next to each numeral are Algerian Eye stitched in DMC 823 (see page 126).

6 When the stitching is complete, check for missed stitches and press on the wrong side. If using a purchased clock kit, make as instructed by the manufacturer. To complete as illustrated, stretch and mount the stitching (see Materials and General Techniques, page 128). Using sharp scissors, pierce the hole for the spindle from the *right* side of the work, fit the spindle and hands and frame as desired.

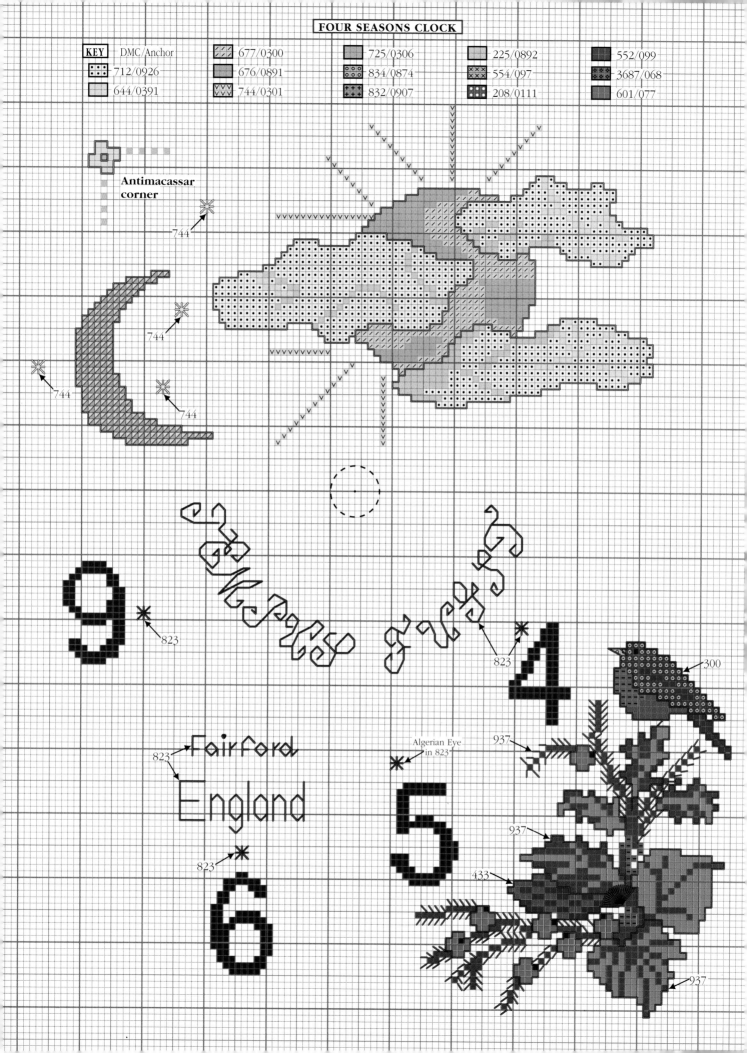

FOUR SEASONS CLOCK

KEY — DMC/Anchor

712/0926	677/0300	725/0306	225/0892	552/099
644/0391	676/0891	834/0874	554/097	3687/068
	744/0301	832/0907	208/0111	601/077

Antimacassar corner

744

744

744

744

823

823

823

823

823

Algerian Eye
in 823

937

937

937

433

300

9

4

5

6

Fairford

England

ANTIQUE KEY CUPBOARD

This unusual design was inspired by the need to find a home for my antique key collection gathering dust on the hall table. In the end, the antique keys stayed put and our house and car keys filled the hooks inside the stitched cupboard.

There are a number of excellent cabinet-makers producing wooden boxes (see Acknowledgements) similar to the lovely one illustrated in the picture, although the dimensions of the design or rebate will obviously vary. The maximum design size for the pine-coloured box in the photograph is 8inches (20.5cm) square and the dimensions and instructions for this project correspond to that. Before starting the project, purchase the cupboard, check the rebate and, if necessary, adapt my design accordingly.

Design size: 7¼inches (18.5cm) square
Stitch count: 92 x 93

10 x 10inches (25.5 x 25.5cm) Zweigart Dublin linen, 25/26 threads per inch (2.5cm)
Stranded cottons (floss), as listed on the chart

1 Work a narrow hem around the edge of the linen to prevent fraying. Fold the linen in four, press lightly and mark the folds with a line of tacking (basting) stitches.
2 Following the chart, work the cross stitch starting in the centre, using two strands for the cross stitch and one for the back stitch outline.
3 The outline colours are suggested on the chart.
4 When the cross stitch is complete, check for missed stitches, then press lightly on the wrong side.
5 Refer to the section on stretching and mounting in Materials and General Techniques (pages 128–30) and complete the cupboard by following the manufacturer's instructions.

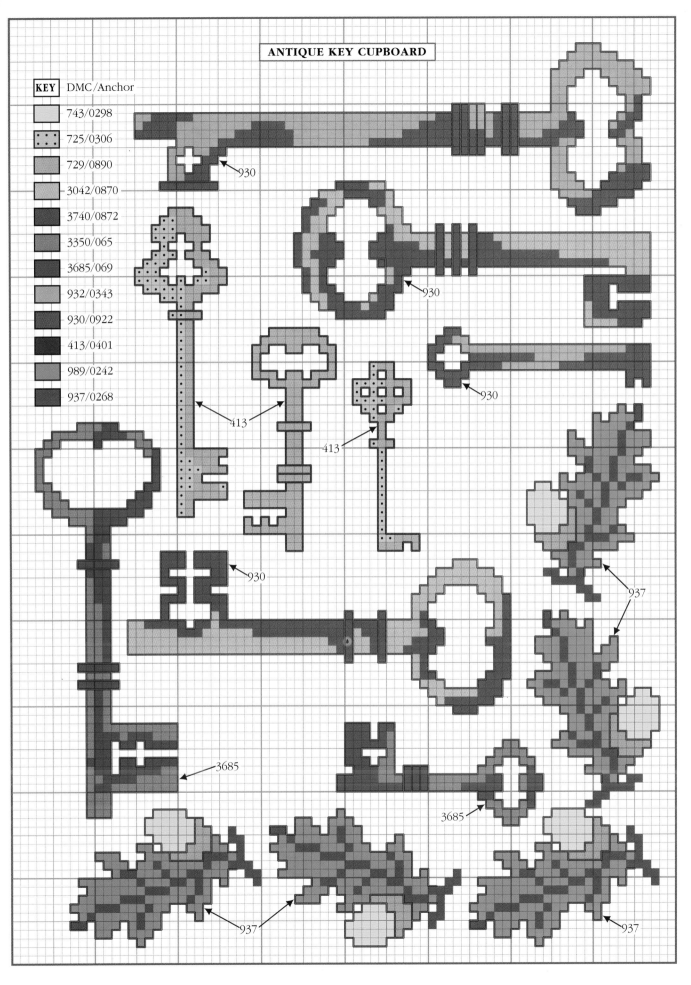

ANTIQUE KEY CUPBOARD

KEY	DMC/Anchor
	743/0298
	725/0306
	729/0890
	3042/0870
	3740/0872
	3350/065
	3685/069
	932/0343
	930/0922
	413/0401
	989/0242
	937/0268

2

THE FAMILY ROOM

THE FAMILY ROOM

*In our small cottage, an open fire, the easy chair where I stitch on wintry evenings,
my husband's piano and bookcases full of treasures old and
new are what makes our family room something special.*

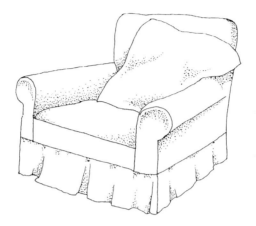

BANDED CUSHIONS

All the lovely cushions pictured on the previous page were based on an idea I saw in Germany, where linen bands (see Materials and General Techniques, page 122) are used to decorate table linen and dresser shelves, and to add cross stitch detail to cushions. The simplest ideas are often the most effective, as you can see from the photograph. I have used patterned fabric and where possible have echoed the design or colour scheme in cross stitch on a linen band.

1 The designs on each of the cushions in the photograph were made from the charts on pages 22, 23, 50 and 51. Select the patterns you prefer and alter the colourway to suit your background fabric.

2 Measure the cushion pad you intend to use and cut the background fabric, adding 4inches (10cm) to the overall dimension for turnings. The square cushions in the photograph were all based on 12inch pads (30.5cm).

3 To cut the band I allowed 16inches (40 cm) per cushion. I worked my design from the centre of the band in each case, adding outline detail as shown on the chart. In all the examples illustrated I used two strands of stranded cotton (floss) for the cross stitch and one for any back stitch outline.

BINDWEED CUSHION

16inches (40cm) half-bleached linen band with a decorated edge, 4inches (10cm) wide, 28 threads per inch (2.5cm)
Stranded cottons (floss) as listed on the footstool chart on pages 22-3
Background fabric

I have repeated the central motif from the Pastel Bindweed Footstool (pages 22-3), to match the theme in the fabric. When completed, the linen band was stitched across the bottom third of the cushion.

BORAGE AND BOWS

16inches (40cm) bleached linen band with a green edge, 2¾inches (7cm), 28 threads per inch (2.5cm)
Stranded cottons (floss) as listed on the chart on page 51
Plain background fabric
Patterned fabric for the frill

I have repeated the Borage and Bows design from the Scullery chapter to link this lovely glazed cotton background material with the soft cotton frill around the edge.
  When completed, the linen band was stitched diagonally across the top right corner.

CREEPING JENNY CUSHIONS

This design (pages 18-19) is taken from the chart on page 51. Here are two versions using two colourways and two different linen bands.

CUSHION A (FRONT LEFT IN PICTURE)
16 inches (40cm) unbleached plain linen band, 2¾inches (7cm) wide, 28 threads per inch (2.5cm)
Flower print background fabric
Stranded cotton (floss) as listed on the chart on page 51

Stitch the design according to the chart. When stitching is complete, apply the band to the cushion, as shown in the photograph on the opposite page.

CUSHION B (MIDDLE REAR IN PICTURE)
16inches (40cm) bleached linen band with a pink decorative edge, 2¾inches (7cm) wide, 28 threads per inch (2.5cm)
Stranded cotton (floss), as listed on the chart on page 51
Plain background fabric
Patterned fabric for the border

Stitch the design according to the chart. When the cross stitch is complete, apply the band to the plain fabric as shown in the photograph.

BINDWEED ANTIMACASSAR

This simple but effective antimacassar (pages 18-19) could be stitched in one evening. The size of the completed project will depend on the overall measurement across the back of your sofa or armchair. The antimacassar should lie over the back of the supporting cushions at head height. The design is taken from the central section of the footstool, illustrated on page 22, and uses the corner motifs shown on page 14 (top left).

Design size: 4¾ x 2¼inches (10.5 x 6cm)
Stitch count: 66 x 34

Stranded cottons (floss), as listed on the charts on pages 22-3
16 x 28inches (40.5 x 71cm) ivory linen, 28 threads per inch (2.5cm)
2¾yd (2.5m) eyelet band 2inches (5cm) wide, 28 threads per inch (2.5cm)
Offray Designer Ribbon, 0.3cm wide in Dusty Rose and Colonial Rose

1 Cut two pieces of eyelet band 18inches (46cm) long and two pieces 30inches (76cm) long.
2 Lay the linen on a clean flat surface and place the eyelet band on the top of the linen along the edges (see diagram). Turn in the raw edges, pin and tack (baste) in position.
3 Mitre each corner (see diagram) and sew with a sewing machine (or by hand with small running stitches) using matching thread.
4 The cross stitch is centred in the lower half, 5½inches (14cm) from the bottom. I added a simple corner motif where pleasing to the eye. Add the back stitch as indicated on the foot
stool chart overleaf using one strand of stranded cotton (floss).
5 To complete the project, thread the narrow ribbon through the eyelet holes using a large needle. I used the darker shade of pink for the outside line of eyelets. Add a simple bow at each corner and press lightly on the wrong side.

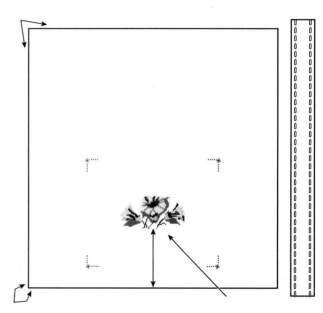

Position of eyelet band on linen, and the position of the cross stitch motifs

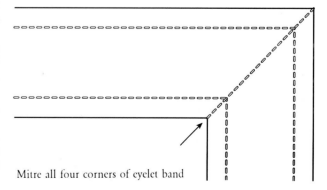

Mitre all four corners of eyelet band

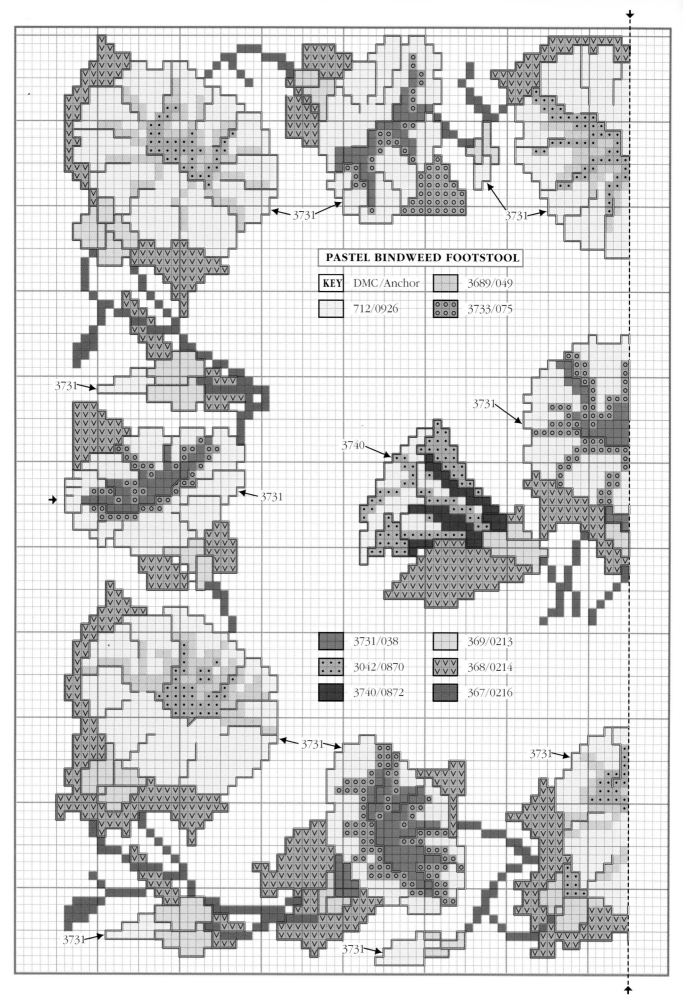

PASTEL BINDWEED FOOTSTOOL

KEY	DMC/Anchor		
	712/0926		3689/049
			3733/075

	3731/038		369/0213
	3042/0870		368/0214
	3740/0872		367/0216

3731

3731

3731

3731

3740

3731

3731

3731

3731

3731

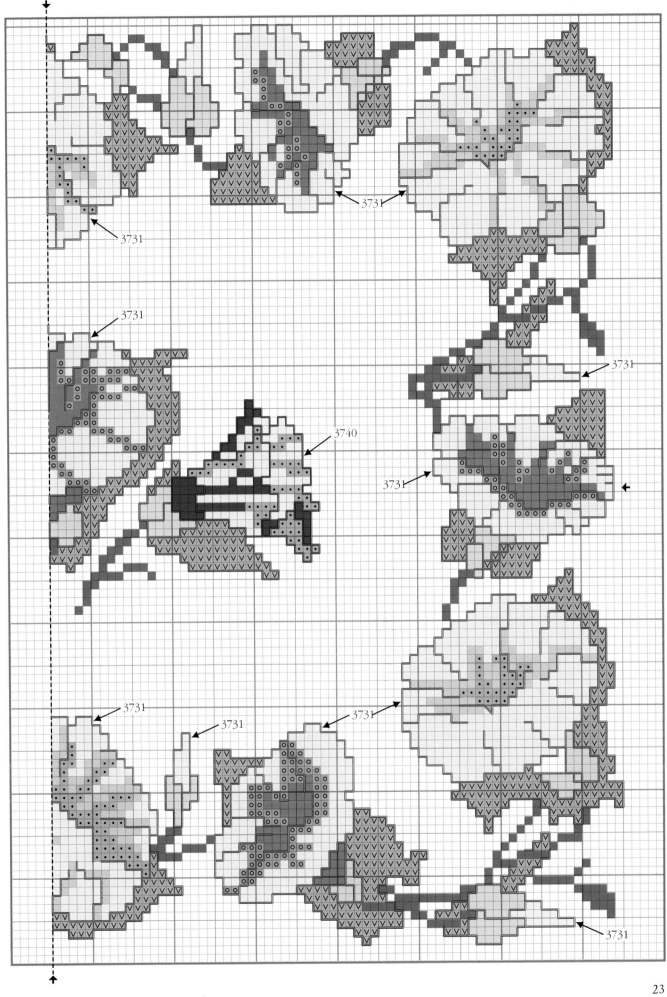

3731

3731

3731

3740

3731

3731

3731

3731

3731

3731

PASTEL BINDWEED FOOTSTOOL

Anybody who knows the Greenoff garden will know that I have a natural affinity with weeds! I have always loved daises, poppies and the lovely soft colours of the bindweed climbing the fence. The pale purple and pink varieties inspired this beautiful footstool design (below), which is also repeated on the antimacassar and one of the banded cushions.

Design size: 14 x 11inches (35 x 28cm)
Stitch count: 140 x 109

Natural linen, 20 threads per inch (2.5cm)
Stranded cottons (floss) as listed on the chart on pages 22-3

1 Carefully check the dimensions of the pad for your choice of footstool and adapt my design where necessary.
2 Cut a piece of linen at least 5inches (13cm) larger than the footstool pad to allow for turnings. Hem to prevent fraying. This is particularly important when using coarse linen, as it *will* fray.
3 Fold in four and mark the folds with a line of tacking (basting) stitches. Starting in the centre of the fabric, work the cross stitch from the chart using three strands of stranded cotton (floss) for the cross stitch and two for the back stitch outline.
4 When the stitching is complete, check for missed stitches and press on the wrong side. Stretch and make up as desired (see Materials and General Techniques on page 132).

THERE'S NO PLACE LIKE HOME

This nostalgic project was inspired by my first purchase of embroidery on stitching paper.

Design size: 15½ x 9½inches (39 x 24cm)
Stitch count: 210 x 133

20 x 14inches (50 x 35.5cm) tea-coloured linen, 28 threads per inch (2.5cm)
Stranded cottons (floss), as listed on the chart on pages 26-7

1 Sew a narrow hem around the edge of the linen to prevent fraying. Fold in four and mark the folds with a line of tacking (basting) stitches. Set aside.

2 Before starting to stitch you will need to plan the layout, (see the section on Planning Your Own Designs on page 127). Using graph paper, copy the outline of the letters and position of the flowers (see chart overleaf). The measurements and stitch counts above refer to the example in the colour photograph opposite.
3 Work the design from the centre using two strands of stranded cotton (floss) for the cross stitch and one for the back stitch outline and pink scroll lines.
4 When the design is complete, check for missed stitches press lightly and frame as preferred (see Materials and General Techniques, page 130).

THERE'S NO PLACE LIKE HOME

KEY	DMC/Anchor		
	744/0301		333/0119
	725/0306		3740/0872
	722/0323		340/0118
	3688/066		3042/0870
	3687/068		3053/0858
	327/0100		3051/0861
			310/0403

MUSIC SAMPLER

This design (see previous page) is a great family favourite. The music at the top and bottom is from *On Wings of Song*, composed by Mendelssohn, and the famous quote 'If music be the food of love...' comes from *Twelfth Night* by William Shakespeare.

This design is not really suited to Aida fabric so choose an even-weave fabric such as linen or Linda. The dimensions below do not include the optional fabric mount.

Design size: 11 x 9inches (28 x 23cm)
Stitch count: 160 x 128

Ivory linen, 28 threads per inch (2.5cm) at least 5inches (13cm)
 larger all round than the finished design
Contrasting linen for mounting the design
Stranded cottons (floss) as listed on the chart opposite

1 Hem the raw edges of the ivory linen to prevent fraying.
2 Fold in four and press lightly. Mark the folds with tacking (basting) stitches. This will also mark the centre.
3 Looking at the chart, starting in the middle of the fabric work the cross stitch, using two strands of stranded cotton (floss) for the cross stitch and one strand for any back stitch outlining unless stated below.
4 The ivory keys on the piano section are left unstitched, but are outlined in one strand of black stranded cotton (floss). If preferred, the keys could be cross stitched using two strands of DMC 712.
5 The staves or manuscript lines are stitched in back stitch using one strand of black. All the musical notes and motifs are stitched in two strands of black.
6 When the cross stitch is complete, add the strings on the drum in back stitch using one strand of the colour indicated. The writing is worked in two strands of blue (DMC 824) with a line of six French knots at the end of the phrase.
7 All the instruments are outlined in one strand of the colour indicated on the chart. Pegs stitched in French knots are added in one strand of black at the end of the finger boards on the violin, the guitar and the cello.
8 Work French knots in one strand of black for the pegs on the harp and to indicate the holes in the recorder. The strings on the harp and the music stand are stitched in back stitch using one strand of grey.
9 Add musical notes to the horn of the gramophone at random.
10 When the cross stitch and outline is complete, press lightly on the wrong side and frame as desired (see Materials and General Techniques, page 130).
11 The design in the colour photograph has a coloured fabric mount, on which I have added a few musical notes in black at random. Please refer to Materials and General Techniques for guidance.

Previous Page: Music Sampler

3

THE
DINING
ROOM

THE DINING ROOM

PURPLE GRAPE TABLE LINEN

This pretty tablecloth and napkin design (see previous page) could be adapted easily to make single place mats if preferred. The purpley-blue and the green grapes are charted on page 36. The motifs can be added singly or in groups to achieve the effect you require.

The cross stitch was worked in two strands of stranded cotton (floss) and the outline added in one strand only. I worked the design on a fine afghan fabric (see Suppliers), but any linen or even-weave fabric would be suitable. Do remember to check that the fabric you have chosen is easy to wash.

POPPY APRON

The Poppy Apron and Pan Holder are perfect for those occasions when you would rather not splash bolognese sauce down your silk shirt, but your real apron and oven mitt are only to be seen by those who love you!

Design size: 5¼ x 4¾inches (13.5 x 12cm)
Stitch count: 76 x 67

Sage Aida, 14 blocks per inch (2.5cm)
Stranded cottons (floss) as listed on the chart on page 37
Purchased satin bias binding (cut your own bias binding if preferred)
Lining fabric or calico if desired

1 Cut out the apron shape in Aida fabric, using the plan on page 133 without the section for the pocket. Overlock the raw edges on a sewing machine to prevent fraying. If you intend to line the apron when complete, cut out the lining at the same time and set aside.

2 Position the design where it most pleases you and, using the chart on page 37, work the large poppy spray using two strands for the cross stitch and one strand for the back stitch outline.
3 To work the seed head, left blank on the chart, work French knots in two strands of dark grey, packing in as many as possible (see More Advanced Stitches on pages 125–6).
4 If you want to decorate your apron further, add more motifs at random, possibly using the smaller flower spray illustrated on the Pan Holder.
5 When the stitching is complete, check for missed stitches and press on the wrong side.
6 Whether you are using a purchased bias binding or making your own, the principles for making up this apron are the same as described for the Gardener's Apron (see page 132). If you wish to line the apron, tack the lining to the wrong side of the project, matching the raw edges, and thereafter follow directions on page 132.

PAN HOLDER

Design size: 3 x 3¾inches (7.5 x 9.5cm)
Stitch count: 40 x 50

Sage Aida, 14 blocks per inch (2.5cm)
Stranded cottons (floss) as listed on the chart on page 37
Purchased satin bias binding (cut your own bias binding if preferred)
Polyester wadding
Two pieces of blanket-weight fabric, 9inches (23cm) square
Lining fabric or calico

1 Cut a piece of sage Aida 41 x 9½inches (104 x 24cm) and sew a line of tacking (basting) stitches 9inches (23cm) from the short edge (see diagram).

2 Find the centre of the sections marked A and work the small poppy motif from the chart twice. In each case the poppy spray is worked with the stems towards the line of tacking (basting) (see diagram), using two strands for the cross stitch and one for the back stitch outline.

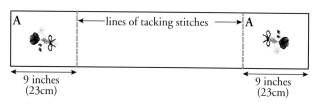

Tacking basting stitches on Pan Holder and the position of the cross stitch

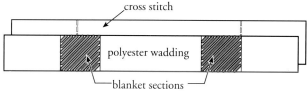

cross stitch

polyester wadding

blanket sections

Position of blanket sections

3 When the stitching is complete, press on the wrong side and make up as follows.
4 Lay the completed cross stitch face down on a clean flat surface, long side facing you. Cut a piece of polyester wadding the same size as the project and place on the wrong side, matching raw edges. Place one piece of blanket fabric in position on top of the polyester wadding, with one edge aligned with the tacking threads (see diagram). Tack (baste) the blanket fabric in position around all four sides.

5 Cut a piece of lining fabric, or calico if preferred, 41 x 9½inches (104 x 24cm) and lay this on top of the now padded Pan Holder.
6 Tack all four sides of the project through all the layers and then add the binding (see Materials and General Techniques, page 133). Stitch the binding to the two short edges, press lightly and then fold the bound edge on the line of tacking (basting) and pin in position (see diagram). Now bind the two long edges, folding in raw ends, and stitch invisibly by hand.

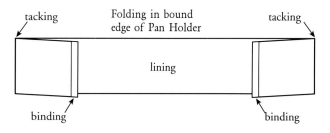

tacking   Folding in bound   tacking
                 edge of Pan Holder

lining

binding   binding

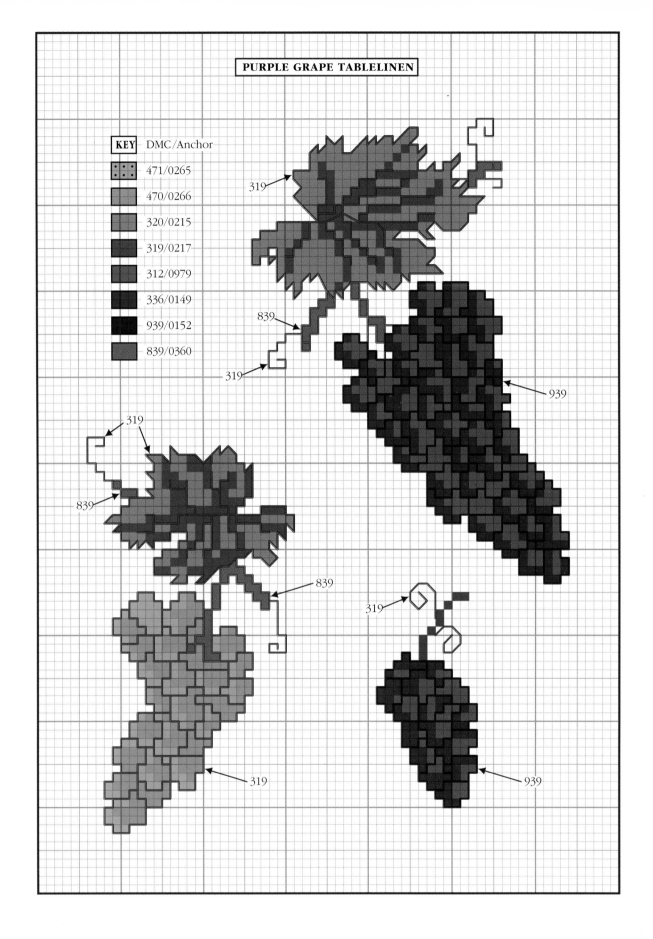

PURPLE GRAPE TABLELINEN

KEY	DMC/Anchor
	471/0265
	470/0266
	320/0215
	319/0217
	312/0979
	336/0149
	939/0152
	839/0360

POPPY SPRAYS

KEY	DMC/Anchor		
	White/01		336/0149
	414/0399		744/0301
	368/0214		742/0303
	367/0216		760/09
	931/0921		3712/010
	312/0979		347/013
			931 + 0336/ 0921 + 0149

336

367

367

367

336

367

FRENCH
KNOTS
IN 414

347

367

367

367

367

742

367

336

336

367

336

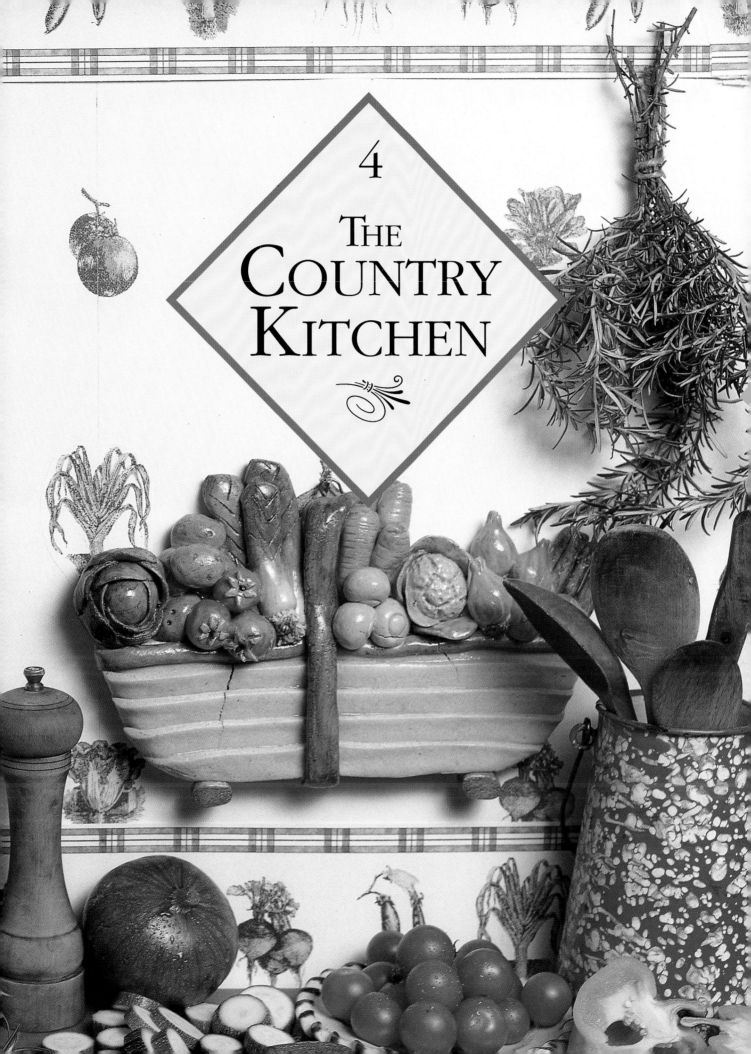

4

THE COUNTRY KITCHEN

THE COUNTRY KITCHEN

Like most wives and mothers I spend a great proportion of my time in the kitchen,
although possibly not making jam, marmalade and home-made bread. I do most of
my thinking in this, our largest room, whether about family or stitching matters.

FRUIT AND VEGETABLE CLOCK

This amusing kitchen project (page 38) uses a purchased perspex clock with a quartz movement (see Suppliers). You could adapt this project to use the puddings charted on page 45 if you prefer.

Finished clock size: 8inches (20cm) square
Design size: 7inches (18cm) square
Stitch count: 98 x 98

12 x 12inches (30.5 x 30.5cm) cream Aida, 14 blocks per inch (2.5cm)
Stranded cottons (floss), as listed on the charts on pages 42-3
8inch (20.5cm) perspex clock kit

1 Using a sheet of graph paper, plan the layout of the clock face using the numerals on page 43. Choose the fruit and/or a vegetable from the chart and place alongside the numbers in a pleasing position (refer to Materials and General Techniques, page 127).
2 Work a narrow hem around the edge of the Aida to prevent fraying.
3 Use two strands of stranded cotton (floss) for the cross stitch and one strand for any back stitch outlining and the clock numerals. You will see that in some cases two shades of stranded cotton are combined (see Tweeding on page 127).
4 When the stitching is complete, check for missed stitches and press lightly on the wrong side.
5 To make up, follow the manufacturer's instructions.

FOOD, GLORIOUS FOOD!

This design for a sampler uses a combination of garlic and mushroom motifs to form a border (all motifs are charted on pages 42-4). The border motifs are shown right-handed and left-handed to assist your planning efforts.

Design size: 14 x 22inches (35.5 x 56cm)
Stitch count: 138 x 220

20 x 27inches (50 x 68cm) unbleached linen, 20 threads per inch (2.5cm)
Stranded cottons (floss), as listed on the charts on pages 42, 43 and 44

1 Plan the layout as described in Planning Your Own Designs on page 127. Add the cheese, fruit and vegetables using the colour picture as a guide and then add the border.

Remember, when planning a design, you only need copy the outline of each motif on to your graph paper, then stitch the designs from the colour charts in the book.
2 Work a narrow hem around the edge to prevent fraying. This is very important with coarse fabrics as they really do fray! Fold the fabric in four and mark the folds with lines of tacking (basting) stitches to mark the centre.
3 In the design in the photograph I stitched the word 'Food' above my central point, with the selection of cheeses underneath.
4 I worked the cross stitch using three strands of stranded cotton (floss) for the cross stitch, and the back stitch outlines using two strands in the colour indicated on the chart.
5 When the cross stitch is complete, check for missed stitches and frame as preferred (see Materials and General Techniques, page 130).

COUNTRY KITCHEN

611

840

611

840

937

840

304

989

930

611

304

937

3685

840

930

KEY	DMC/Anchor
△△△	Blanc/01
	712/926
⊚⊚⊚	744/0301
	725/306
⊙⊙⊙	472/278
	612/0832
	471/265
VVV	989/0261
	320/215
	937/0263
	677/0300
◇◇◇	738/0372
∧∧∧	676/0891
	977/313
	722/323
∥∥∥	841/0378
	729/0891
∙∙∙	611/0832
	840/0379

543/0933
353/06
321/9046
309/042
304/047
326/059
3350/0896
3685/0897
3033/0388
3032/0392
3042/0870
3041/0871
327/0872
930/0922
353 + 471/
06 + 265
3350 + 472/
0896 + 278

937
611
729
989
840
937
937
937
840
611
937
3685
611
840

1 2 3 4 5 6
7 8 9 10 11 12

937
840

3685
3350

KEY DMC/Anchor
△△△ Blanc/01
712/926
3033/0388

3032/0392
729/0891
321/9046
304/047

326/059
3041/0871
317/0400
677/0300

738/0372
676/0891
840/0379
611/0832

317

304

317

317

317

ALL WAVY
LINES IN 840
ONE STRAND

PUDDINGS

898

898

632

898

632

One strand half stitch 309

One strand half stitch 309

436

632

898

632

898

898

632

898

632

414

PUDDINGS

This design makes me smile every time I stitch it, as I have an allergy to cream, and so this is the closest I can come to puddings!

Design size: 10½ x 9½inches (27 x 24cm)
Stitch count: 138 x 119

15 x 14inches (38 x 35cm) marshmallow pink linen, 28 threads per inch (2.5cm)
Stranded cottons (floss) as listed on the chart on page 45

1 Fold the linen in four and mark the folds with tacking (basting) stitches. Sew a narrow hem to prevent fraying. Set aside while you plan your design.
2 My version of the Puddings sampler uses an alphabet from page 121 with the delicious puddings and cakes arranged around the edge (see Planning Your Own Designs on page 127).
3 The cross stitch was stitched using two strands of stranded cotton (floss) and the outline added using one strand only in the colour indicated on the chart. To achieve the see-through effect, the jelly in the ice cream sundae in the centre was stitched in one strand of stranded cotton (floss), in half cross stitch only.
4 When the stitching is complete, check for missed stitches, press lightly and frame as preferred (see Materials and General Techniques, page 130).

5

THE
SCULLERY

The Scullery

One of my earliest childhood memories is looking up to the white scullery sink, whilst an enamel bowl was filled with cold water and bubbles, so that I could wash my doll's clothes. What a useful room, cold enough to store things and somewhere to hide the ironing!

Wash-day Peg Bag

A simple but really useful project (see previous page) based on a small wooden coat hanger. The project is made up in two sections, one including a line of washing, and a back section decorated with four clothes pegs.

The stitch count and design size refer to the line of washing on the bottom section of the peg bag. Any number of clothes pegs may be added to the top section.

Completed peg bag size: 12inches (30.5cm) square
Design size: 6¾ x 3¼inches (17 x 8.5cm)
Stitch count: 94 x 44

Lemon Aida, 14 blocks per inch (2.5cm)
Stranded cottons (floss), as listed on the chart
Patterned fabric or bias binding
Coat hanger
Calico fabric for the back lining

1 To determine the finished size of the peg bag, select a suitable wooden coat hanger. The following instructions are based on a coat hanger 11inches (28cm) wide. Adapt your measurements to suit.

2 Cut a piece of Aida fabric 14 x 10inches (35.5 x 25.5cm) and set aside. Cut another piece of Aida 14 x 7inches (35.5 x 18cm) for the back section.

3 Fold the larger piece of fabric in four, press lightly, and mark the folds with a line of tacking (basting) stitches. Looking at the chart begin stitching, placing the small white handkerchief (the centre of the line of washing) 3½inches (9cm) down from the top edge, but on the centre line. Following the chart, work the remainder of the washing using two strands of stranded cotton (floss) for the cross stitch and one strand for the back stitch outlining. Set aside.

4 Fold the smaller section in four and mark the folds as above.

5 Work the clothes pegs either side of the centre line, placing them in a pleasing position.

6 When the cross stitch is complete, check for missed stitches. To complete the peg bag, press and make up as described in Materials and General Techniques on page 131.

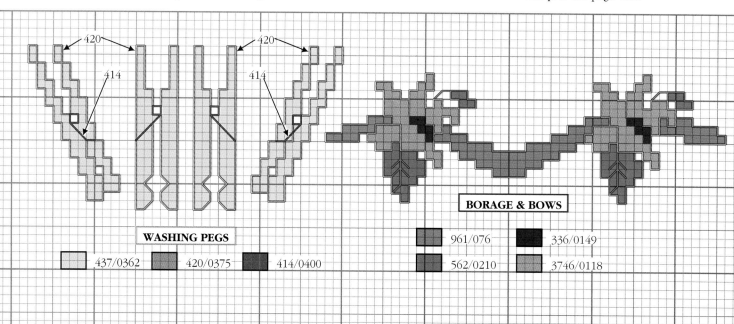

WASHING PEGS

	437/0362		420/0375		414/0400

BORAGE & BOWS

	961/076		336/0149
	562/0210		3746/0118

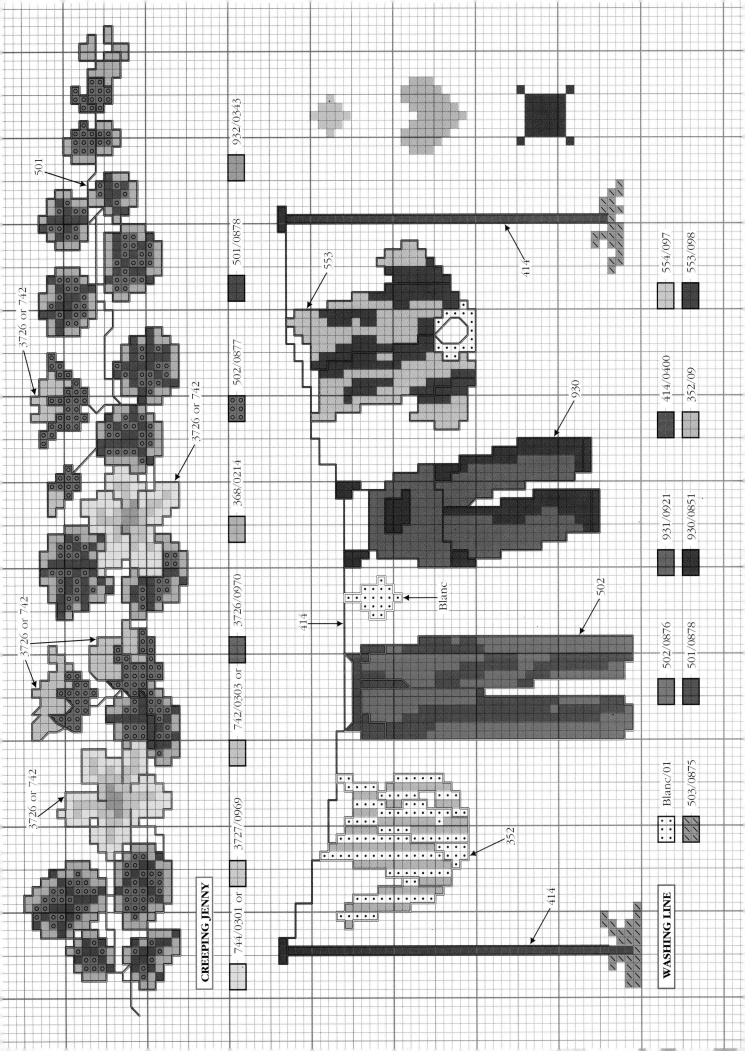

CREEPING JENNY

501

3726 or 742

3726 or 742

3726 or 742

3726 or 742

3726 or 742

3726 or 742

744/0301 or	3727/0969
742/0303 or	3726/0970
368/0214	502/0877
501/0878	932/0343

553

414

930

Blanc

414

502

352

414

414

WASHING LINE

Blanc/01	503/0875
502/0876	501/0878
931/0921	930/0851
414/0400	352/09
554/097	553/098

LINEN BANDS

These bands (see page 48) are the perfect answer to the muddle at the back of the airing cupboard.

Pillowcase – *ivory eyelet band 3¼inches (8cm) wide, 28 threads per inch (2.5cm)*
Linen – *ivory decorated-edge band, 2¼inches (6cm) wide, 28 threads per inch (2.5cm)*
Towels – *half-bleached decorated band, 2¼ (6cm) wide, 28 threads per inch (2.5cm)*
Stranded cottons (floss)

Narrow ribbon in cream, yellow or blue to trim linen band

1 Use the alphabets at the back of the book, working each letter down the length of the linen band.
2 Add any suitable motifs to decorate the band, check for missed stitches and press lightly.
3 Fold the raw edges to the wrong side forming a point, hem invisibly and add the ribbon ties with matching thread.

Soap Hanger

SOAP HANGER

1 Use the linen band as above, but work one of the floral designs from the chart chosen to match the family soap. I stitched a yellow version of the design used for the Creeping Jenny Cushions, using two strands of stranded cotton (floss) for the cross stitch and one for the back stitch outline.

2 When the cross stitch is complete, press lightly.
3 Turn the raw edges to the wrong side to form a point and hem invisibly.
4 Add two brass rings to each end, fill with soaps and hang from a cup hook.

ODD SOCK SACK

This simple project can be stitched in one evening and is so useful! The design is stitched on a piece of linen band selected to match the linen background fabric. Using linen band enables you to add cross stitch to almost anything.

To work the Odd Sock Sack as illustrated, I used the alphabet on page 120 and two pattern repeats from Borage and Bows.

Patterned background fabric 36 x 17inches (92 x 43cm)
Unbleached linen band 2¾inches (7cm) wide, 28 threads per inch (2.5cm)
Stranded cottons (floss) as listed on the chart on page 50

1 Before stitching, copy out the letters you wish to use on to graph paper, adjusting the spacing until you are satisfied. Add the Borage and Bows motif at either end and then mark the centre of the chart.
2 Fold the linen band in half, press lightly. Begin stitching from the centre of your chart and the fold on the linen band.
3 In this project I have not outlined the flowers and have excluded the green leaves. This pretty repeating pattern is shown in detail on a cushion on pages 18-19.
4 For making up, refer to Materials and General Techniques, page 130.

CLEANLINESS IS NEXT TO GODLINESS

This project has a lovely nostalgic feel to it, and some of the motifs remind me of my childhood. The coarse unbleached linen used is ideal for a newcomer to linen, as it is easy to count.

Design size: 15½ x 9½inches (39 x 24cm)
Stitch count: 152 x 96
20½ x 14½inches (52 x 36.5cm) unbleached linen, 20 threads per inch (2.5cm)
Stranded cottons (floss) as listed on the chart on pages 56-7
Small pearls or pearl-coloured beads
Sharp or beading needle

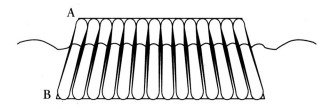

Long stitch and couching

1 Work a narrow hem around the edge to prevent fraying. Fold the fabric in four and press lightly. Mark the folds with a line of tacking (basting) stitches, thus marking the centre.
2 Look at the photograph and referring to the section on Planning Your Own Designs on page 127, select the motifs you wish to include in your design. My version in the colour photograph was stitched on coarse linen so I used three strands of stranded cotton (floss) for the cross stitch and two strands for the outline.
3 Use a long stitch to work the broom and the floor brush as illustrated in the colour photograph. Thread the needle with four strands of stranded cotton (floss) and, looking at the diagram, work long stitches from point A to point B for each brush, ensuring that the fabric is covered and that the thread is not pulled too tight.
4 When the brush shape has been formed, thread your needle with two strands of brown thread and couch the long

stitches down across the width of the broom (see diagram).
5 To work the dandelion head, outline the shape of the fluffy seed head with one strand of stranded cotton (floss) in any pale colour. This will not be visible once the stitching is finished.
6 Thread your needle with three strands of stranded cotton (floss) and starting at the outside (near your outline stitches) begin to work French knots, packing them into the space. You do not need to count this section (see More Advanced Stitches on pages 125-6). As you stitch, add the single beads at random intervals with a half cross stitch in amongst the knots, using a sharp needle. Look at the colour photograph to check as you proceed. As you reach the left-hand centre of the seed head, leave some of the fabric showing to account for the down in the breeze (see small photograph, page 126).
7 When the stitching is complete, check for missed stitches and frame as desired (see Materials and General Techniques, page 130).

Overleaf: Cleanliness is next to Godliness

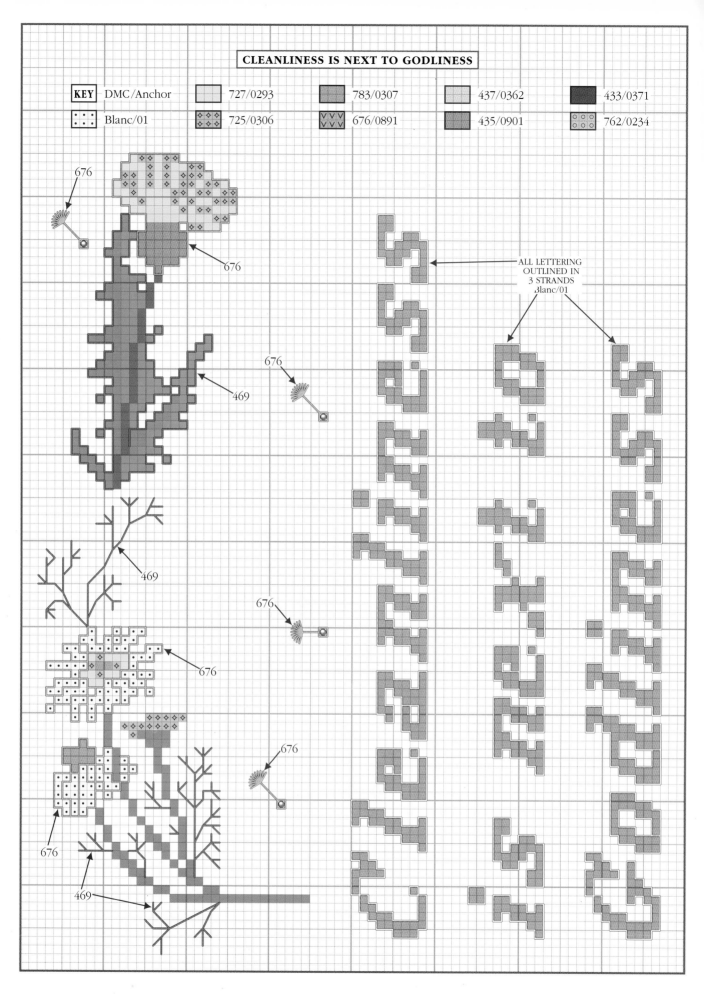

CLEANLINESS IS NEXT TO GODLINESS

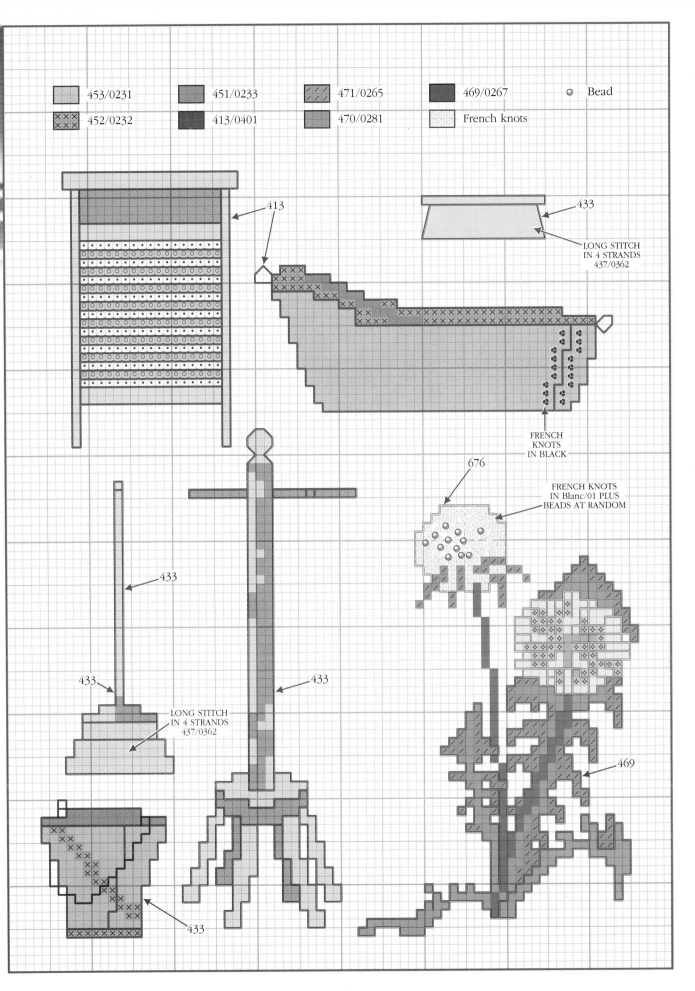

453/0231

452/0232

451/0233

413/0401

471/0265

470/0281

469/0267

Bead

French knots

413

433

LONG STITCH
IN 4 STRANDS
437/0362

FRENCH
KNOTS
IN BLACK

676

FRENCH KNOTS
IN Blanc/01 PLUS
BEADS AT RANDOM

433

433

433

LONG STITCH
IN 4 STRANDS
437/0362

469

433

6

THE
GARDEN

THE GARDEN

This chapter is pure fantasy. I dream of a leafy conservatory, full of dark secret corners, the sound of gently trickling water and scented vines, a pretty table in a corner set with glasses for two and the moon peeping through arched windows. None of this is very likely, as the garden to our cottage is very small, but we do have a vine which produces lovely grapes, a pond with eight tiny goldfish and a herb garden the size of a cardboard box! All the designs in this chapter are based on the charts on pages 61, 64 and 65 and can be adapted to suit a garden planner, an apron, a notebook and the Garden Sampler.

PLANTING PLANNER

This fun project (see previous page) can include all the things you need for your garden.

Parchment Aida, 14 blocks per inch (2.5cm)
Stranded cottons (floss), as listed on the charts on pages 61 and 64
One sheet of acetate overlay

1 Select the motifs you wish to include in the design and map these out on graph paper as described in Planning Your Own Designs on page 127.

2 Work the cross stitch using two strands of stranded cotton (floss), with one strand for the back stitch outline. The solid lines dividing up the fabric are stitched in two strands of dark green, with the writing in one strand only. Refer to the additional instructions for the Garden Sampler for more detail.

3 When the stitching is complete, frame as desired (see Materials and General Techniques, page 130), but without using glass. Cut a piece of acetate overlay to cover the area you will need to write on and fix to the design, using two big drawing pins. This makes it simple to remove the acetate to wipe clean as necessary.

GARDEN SAMPLER

The Garden Sampler (see pages 62-3) was a real labour of love, reflecting my feelings for the garden and my anticipation of stitching the design. All the elements in the design were selected for a personal reason. The wild rose border reminds me of the Cotswold hedgerows, buzzing with bees and butterflies. The topiary trees are reminiscent of the trimmed trees at Sudeley Castle and my weeping rose, sadly now only a memory since the gales.

This large project is not suitable for a complete beginner because you will need to plan the layout before you

start stitching. (Refer to Planning Your Own Designs on page 127.)

Design size: 20 x 14½inches (50 x 36.5cm)
Stitch count: 286 x 201

25 x 20inches (62.5 x 50cm) ivory linen, 28 threads per inch (2.5cm)
Stranded cottons (floss), as listed on the charts on pages 64-5

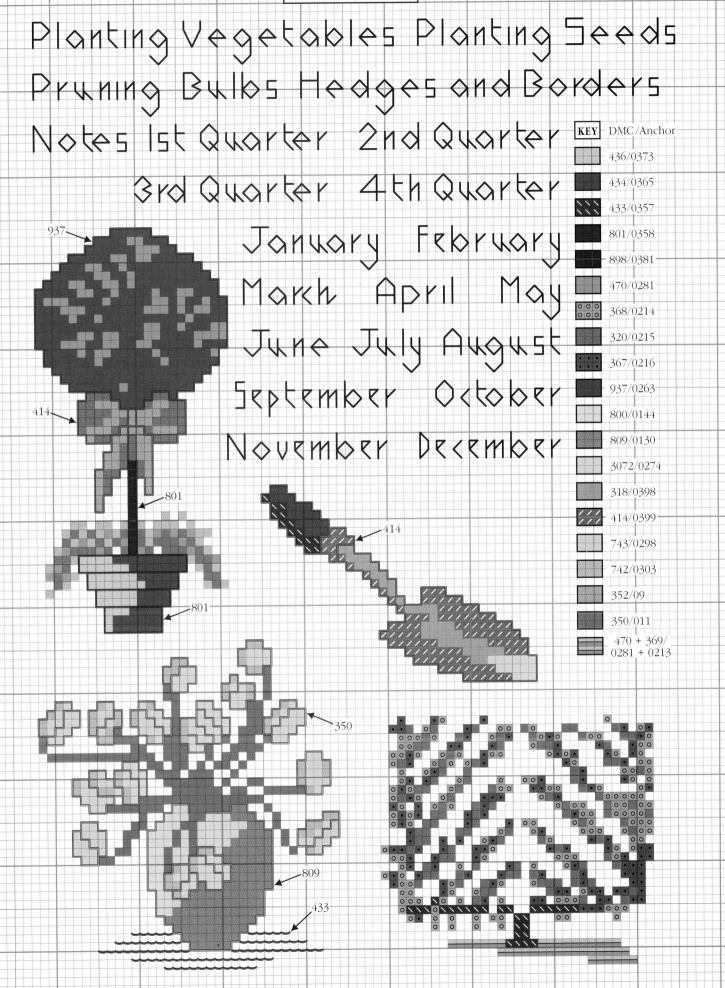

Planting Vegetables Planting Seeds
Pruning Bulbs Hedges and Borders
Notes 1st Quarter 2nd Quarter
3rd Quarter 4th Quarter
January February
March April May
June July August
September October
November December

KEY	DMC/Anchor
	436/0373
	434/0365
	433/0357
	801/0358
	898/0381
	470/0281
	368/0214
	320/0215
	367/0216
	937/0263
	800/0144
	809/0130
	3072/0274
	318/0398
	414/0399
	743/0298
	742/0303
	352/09
	350/011
	470 + 369/ 0281 + 0213

937
414
801
801
414
350
809
433

1 Fold the linen in four and mark the folds with a line of tacking (basting) stitches. Work a narrow hem to prevent fraying and set aside.

2 Refer to the section on Planning Your Own Designs on page 127 and select the garden motifs from the charts on pages 61, 64 and 65. Copy the outlines of the motifs and border repeats on to your master chart as described, adding as much detail as you feel necessary. When you are sure of the position of each motif it can be stitched from the colour charts.

3 When the layout is complete, mark the centre of the chart and working from the middle, begin to stitch, using two strands of stranded cotton (floss) for the cross stitch and one for the back stitch outline.

4 After working the border as illustrated on the chart, fill the blank areas with cross stitch in DMC 712, then add French knots at random for the flower centres (see More Advanced Stitches on pages 125-6).

Add the outline colours in back stitch using the colours indicated on the chart.

6 Add random French knots to the small flower pot in the top left-hand corner in DMC 350 using two strands, and to the spout of the watering can in DMC 310.

7 All the back stitch outlines are added after the cross stitch is complete, using one strand of the colour indicated on the chart. The poem is stitched in two strands of stranded cotton (floss) in back stitch.

8 Mount and frame as described in Materials and General Techniques, 128-30.

TOPIARY TWIST NOTEBOOK

This simple but effective motif was stitched on cream Aida material, 14 blocks per inch (2.5cm), and inserted into a purchased notebook (see pages 58-9). If you wish, any of the garden motifs could be worked on a notebook cover, for the Fisherman's Log Book, page 99 (see Materials and General Techniques, page 129).

GARDENER'S APRON

This lovely project is based on the apron shape and instructions given on page 133, including a useful pocket. The apron was cut out from brown/green linen, 28 threads per inch (2.5cm) and made up using a strong green bias binding to finish the raw edges.

The cross stitch motifs were added at random from the charts on pages 64-5, using two strands for the cross stitch and one for the back stitch outlining.

Garden Sampler

KEY DMC/Anchor

⠿	712/0926
	436/0373
	434/0365
⧄	433/0357
	801/0358
	898/0381
	369/0213
	470/0281
⊙⊙	368/0214
	320/0215
⠿	367/0216
	937/0263
⠿	936/0846
	800/0144
	809/0130
	3072/0274
	318/0398
⧄	414/0399
	413/0401
	310/0403
	743/0298
	742/0303
	353/06
	352/09
	350/011
⊙⊙	369 + 320/ 0213 + 0215
	470 + 369/ 0281 + 0213
	936 + 898/ 0846 + 0381

The kiss of the sun for pardon, The song of the birds for mirth, One is nearer God's heart in a garden, than anywhere else on earth Dorothy Gurney

STITCH ALL LETTERS IN POEM IN 367 ONE STRAND ONLY

350

937

937

310

434

414

434

436

GARDEN SAMPLER

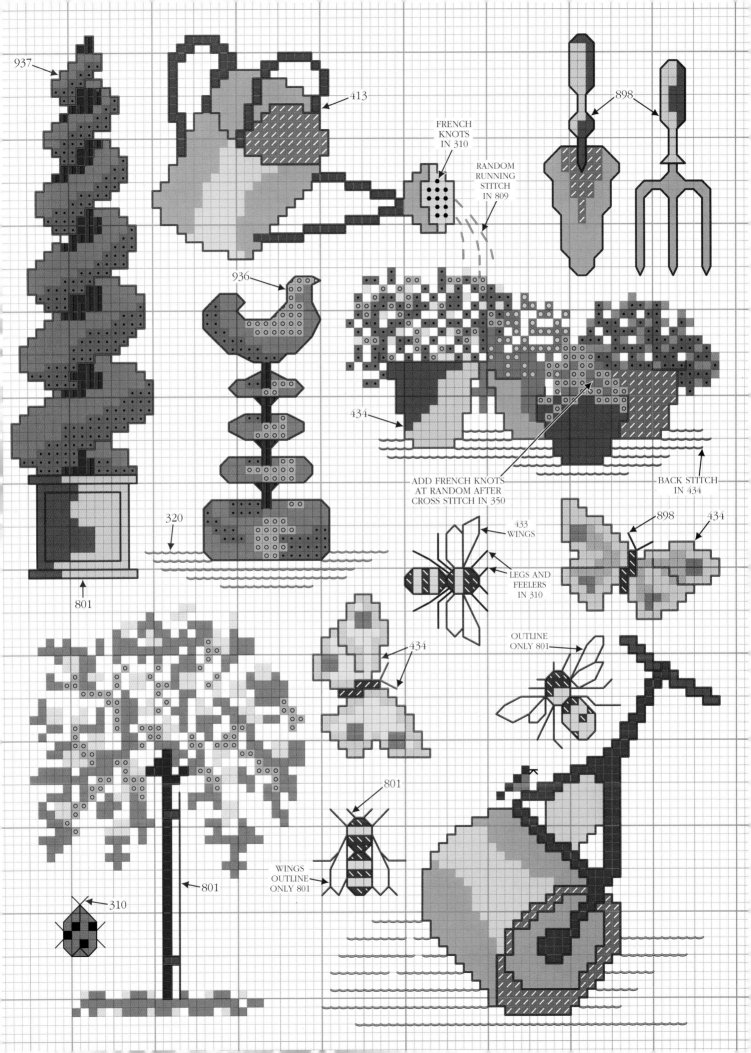

937

413

FRENCH
KNOTS
IN 310

RANDOM
RUNNING
STITCH
IN 809

898

936

434

801

320

ADD FRENCH KNOTS
AT RANDOM AFTER
CROSS STITCH IN 350

BACK STITCH
IN 434

898

434

433
WINGS

LEGS AND
FEELERS
IN 310

434

OUTLINE
ONLY 801

801

801

WINGS
OUTLINE
ONLY 801

310

7
BATH TIME

BATH TIME

My children are enchanted by the sea and have always collected shells, driftwood, pebbles and anything else they could smuggle into the car. It was their idea to have a seaside bathroom in our cottage, with shell wallpaper, seaweed and starfish stencils on the tiles and floorboards and the Seaside Sampler pictured on pages 72 and 73. This chapter is based on the coloured charts on pages 69, 70-1. All the motifs included in the worked examples in the coloured photographs are charted and you can use them to make up your own projects.

SEASHELL HOLDALL

This attractive and useful project (see pages 66 and 67) can be constructed to hang on the back of the bathroom door, if wall space is at a premium. I have used wooden dowelling rod instead of purchased bell-pull hangers, the ends finished with scented wooden balls.

Design size: 17 x 31inches (43 x 79cm)
Background fabric size: 19 x 36inches (48 x 92cm)

20 inches (50cm) pale-grey damask Aida, 14 blocks per inch (2.5cm)
19 x 36inches (48 x 92cm) jade green linen, 28 threads per inch (2.5cm)
Stranded cottons (floss), as listed on the charts on pages 69, 70-71
Assorted shells drilled with one tiny hole
Beads in co-ordinating colours
Sharp or beading needle
Dowelling rod
Four scented wooden balls

1 First plan the layout of the pockets. Looking at the colour photograph decide on the size and number of your pockets and, using brown paper, make and cut the pocket patterns.
2 Lay the pocket patterns on the background fabric and arrange them until you have a pleasing shape.
3 Mark the position of the paper patterns on the background fabric and, using the patterns as templates, cut the damask Aida pockets, allowing at least 1inch (2.5cm) all the way round for turnings.

Prevous page: Seashell Holdall

4 Fold a narrow hem around all four edges of each pocket, tucking in the raw ends. Tack (baste) the hems in position and press lightly.
5 Looking at the seaside charts and the colour photograph, select the motifs you prefer and stitch them on the pockets using the stranded cottons (floss), as indicated on the chart. Refer to the instructions for the Seaside Sampler for additional guidance.
6 When the designs are complete, press lightly on the wrong side.
7 Place the pockets on the background fabric pin and tack (baste) in position.
8 Add any further motifs to the background fabric in the gaps in between the pocket shapes, as shown in the colour photograph.
9 Press on the wrong side and make up as follows.
10 Fold a narrow hem down each side of the holdall and stitch with a sewing machine or by hand, using small running stitches. At the top and bottom of the holdall you will need to form a sleeve for the dowelling rod hanger. Fold the hem and stitch, leaving the ends open.
11 Using matching thread, sew each pocket in position, leaving the top open in each case.
12 Refer to the version of the project on page 66 and add the drilled shells. Attach them by using a sharp needle and one strand of matching thread.
13 Cut the dowelling rod with a small saw at least 2inches (5cms) longer than the width of the holdall. Drill holes in the wooden balls large enough for the dowelling to fit snugly. Slide the dowelling through the sleeve at the top of the holdall and fit the wooden balls on each end. Repeat this procedure for the bottom section.
14 Fill with bathroom goodies and hang behind the bathroom door.

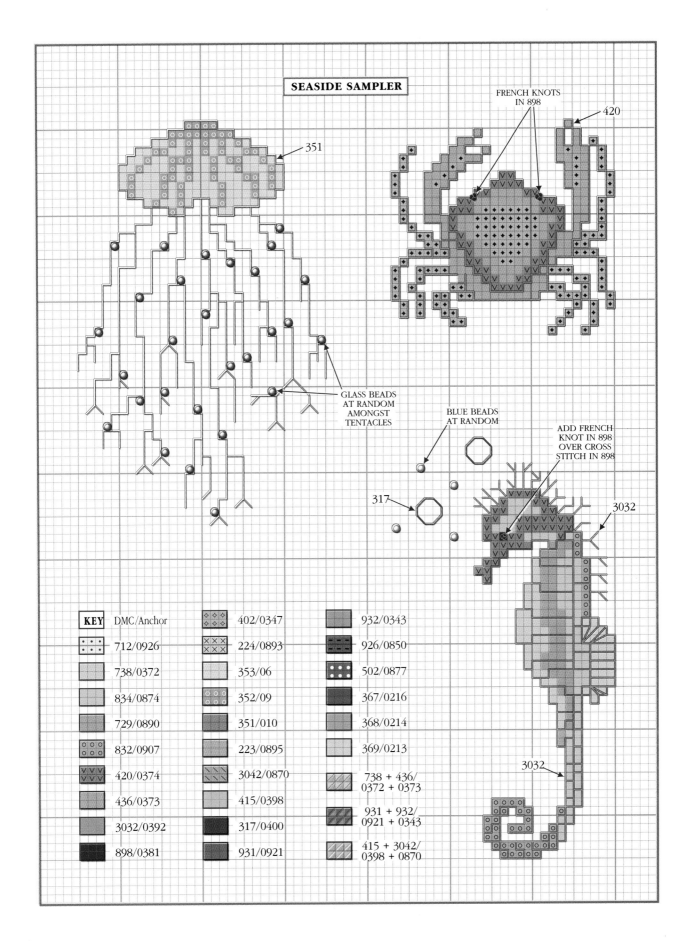

SEASIDE SAMPLER

351

FRENCH KNOTS
IN 898

420

GLASS BEADS
AT RANDOM
AMONGST
TENTACLES

BLUE BEADS
AT RANDOM

ADD FRENCH
KNOT IN 898
OVER CROSS
STITCH IN 898

317

3032

3032

KEY	DMC/Anchor				
	712/0926		402/0347		932/0343
	738/0372		224/0893		926/0850
	834/0874		353/06		502/0877
	729/0890		352/09		367/0216
	832/0907		351/010		368/0214
	420/0374		223/0895		369/0213
	436/0373		3042/0870		738 + 436/ 0372 + 0373
	3032/0392		415/0398		931 + 932/ 0921 + 0343
	898/0381		317/0400		415 + 3042/ 0398 + 0870
			931/0921		

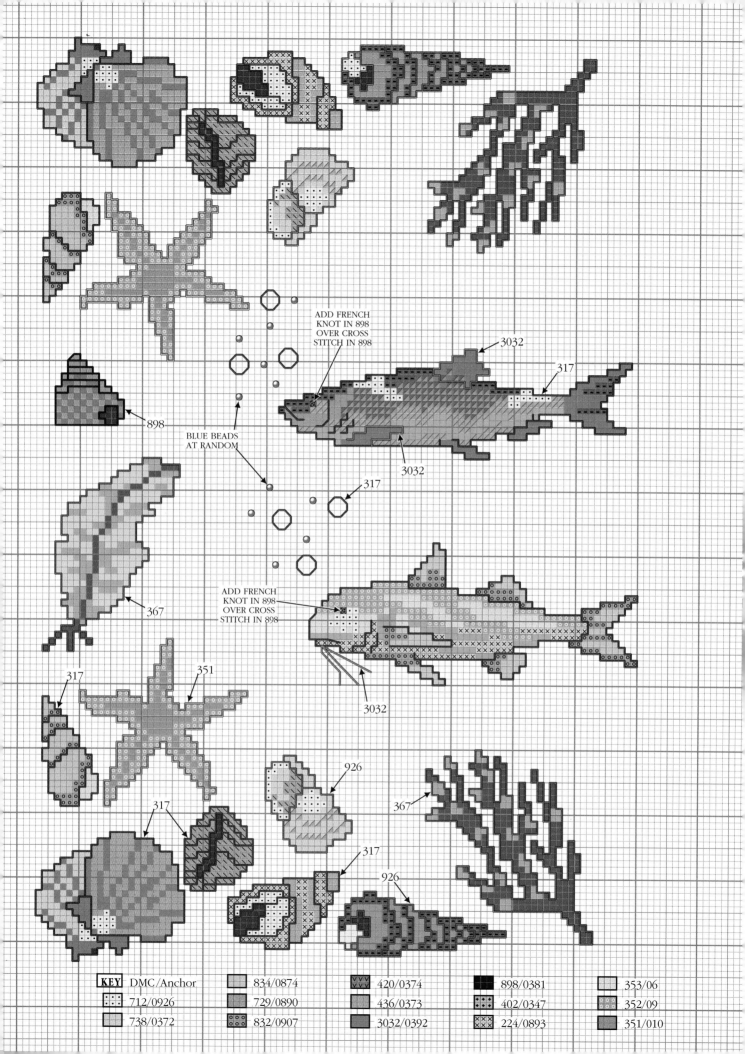

ADD FRENCH
KNOT IN 898
OVER CROSS
STITCH IN 898

3032

317

898

BLUE BEADS
AT RANDOM

3032

317

ADD FRENCH
KNOT IN 898
OVER CROSS
STITCH IN 898

367

317

317

351

926

367

317

926

317

3032

KEY	DMC/Anchor		834/0874		420/0374		898/0381		353/06
	712/0926		729/0890		436/0373		402/0347		352/09
	738/0372		832/0907		3032/0392		224/0893		351/010

317

ADD FRENCH
KNOT IN 898
OVER CROSS
STITCH IN 898

317

BLUE BEADS
AT RANDOM

ADD FRENCH
KNOT IN 898
OVER CROSS
STITCH IN 898

317

SEASIDE SAMPLER
See page 69 for
central motifs

	223/0895		317/0400		926/0850		368/0214		931 + 932/ 0921 + 0343
	3042/0870		931/0921		502/0877		369/0213		415 + 3042/ 0398 + 0870
	415/0398		932/0343		367/0216		738 + 436/ 0372 + 0373		

SEASHELL TOWELS

These lovely soft towels (see pages 67 and 68) are designed especially for cross stitch (see Suppliers), but you can achieve the same effect using the linen band now available from most good needlework shops.

Select the motifs you like from the charts and, after checking the stitch count, stitch using stranded cottons (floss) as listed on the chart.

SEASIDE SAMPLER

This design is a personal favourite of mine. I love the soft ocean colours, the delicate jellyfish tentacles and the tiny beads added to the bubbles.

Design size: 15¾ x 10inches (40 x 25.5cm)
Stitch count: 220 x 143

20 x 15inches (50 x 38cm) ivory linen, 28 threads per inch (2.5 cm)
Stranded cottons (floss), as listed on the charts on pages 69, 70-1
Small cream and sky-blue beads
Sharp or beading needle

1 Work a narrow hem around the edge of the linen. Fold in four and mark the folds with a line of tacking (basting) stitches. Set aside.
2 Refer to Planning Your Own Designs on page 127 and copy the outline of the motifs on to graph paper. Look at the colour photograph opposite to check the position of the border in relation to the fish and seaweed. Mark the centre of the chart with a soft pencil.
3 When you are satisfied with your design, the motifs can be stitched from the colour charts, beginning at the centre of the design. Use two strands of stranded cotton (floss) for the cross stitch, except for the fins and the tails of the fish, which are stitched in one strand only.
4 Work the body of the jellyfish in one strand of colour as indicated, using half cross stitch to give a transparent effect.
5 The back stitch outline is added next to the motif after the cross stitch, in one strand of the colour indicated, as are the tentacles on the jellyfish. Add the bubbles in one strand of dark-grey stranded cotton (floss) in back stitch.
6 Add the small cream beads at random amongst the tentacles, using matching thread, a half cross stitch and a sharp needle. The blue beads are added at random amongst the bubbles in the same manner.
7 Add the fish and crab eyes in French knots on top of the cross stitch.
8 Mount and frame as described in Material and General Techniques.

Seaside Sampler

8

THE NURSERY

THE NURSERY

I have never forgotten the pleasure of planning and decorating the nursery for our first baby – a tiny room with an air balloon light, a teddy mobile and an elephant quilt, all home-made. The size of the designs in this chapter will all vary, depending on your child's name, height, and your dedication.

ALPHABET EXPRESS

This design (see previous page) is as large or as small as you want it to be. The example in the colour photograph is stitched with my son's name. If you are really ambitious you could work the complete alphabet within the train.

1 I stitched my version on Aida, 11 blocks per inch (2.5cm), but it is not essential to use exactly the same fabric.
2 When planning your design, work out how many coaches you need to complete your name or alphabet (see charts pages 77, 78-9). In all cases check that the final letter will fit in the engine tender – if it doesn't, add an extra coach (for example, 'w' would be too large for the tender).

3 Draw out one example of the coach and then centre each letter within the unstitched area. It is not necessary to draw a coach for every letter.
4 My version, shown in the charts, includes waving clowns sitting in the coaches, the first and last ones waving only one hand. Feel free to adapt this as you wish.
5 The design in the photograph was stitched in three strands of stranded cotton (floss) with the back stitch outline worked in two strands only.
6 Mount and frame as described in Materials and General Techniques on page 130.

AIR BALLOON AFGHAN

This lovely soft shawl (see previous page) could be used on the bed, across the back of a chair or even to wrap up a baby. The designs are all taken from the Air Balloon chart on page 81, also used for the Height Chart. I have worked a pastel version of the air balloons to co-ordinate with the other things in the nursery.
There are many afghan-type fabrics available to stitchers, so it is possible to choose plain or very patterned fabrics for your projects, whichever you prefer (see Suppliers).

1 The design illustrated is worked on a soft washable afghan fabric with a self-coloured simple heart pattern surrounding each design.
2 It is worked over two threads using three strands of stranded cotton (floss) for the cross stitch and two for the outline.
3 When the cross stitch is complete, the edge of the shawl is frayed and knotted. Before fraying the edge, sew a line of machine stitching or small back stitches 2inches (5cm) from the raw edge.
4 Remove the horizontal threads carefully and then, if desired, the frayed ends may be knotted.

THE NURSERY
ALPHABET

KEY | DMC/Anchor
931/0921
807/0168

ABCDE
FGHIJKL
MNOPQ
RSTUV
WXYZ
1234567890.

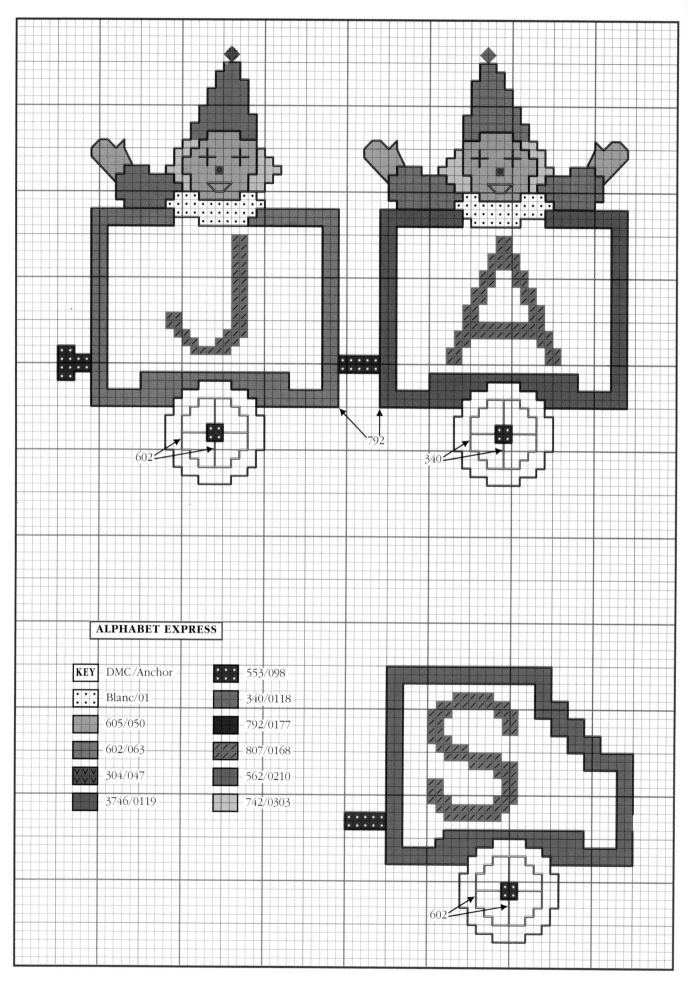

ALPHABET EXPRESS

KEY	DMC/Anchor
	Blanc/01
	605/050
	602/063
	304/047
	3746/0119

	553/098
	340/0118
	792/0177
	807/0168
	562/0210
	742/0303

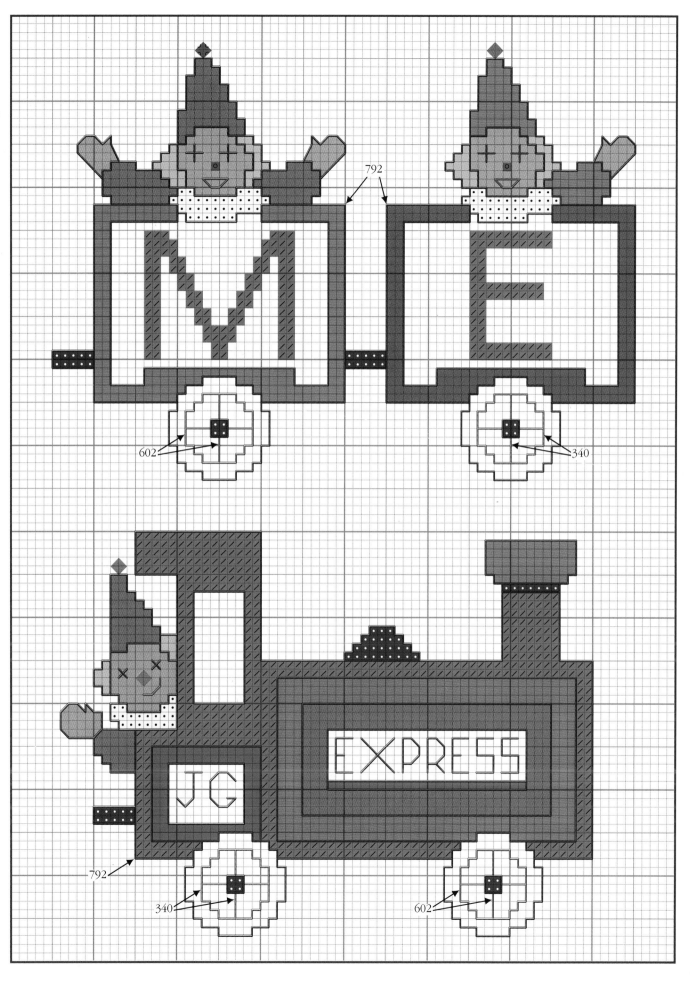

AIR BALLOON HEIGHT CHART

This design (see pages 74-5 is very simple to work, but very effective. The secret is careful measuring at the start.

Before you begin, decide on the size of the finished project and whether you intend to measure in inches or centimetres. The dimensions, stitch counts and instructions below refer to my version, so do remember to adapt as necessary.

Design size: 44 x 7½inches (112 x 19cm)
Stitch count: 440 x 75

Ivory linen, 20 threads per inch (2.5cm)
Stranded cottons (floss), as listed on the chart

1 Cut a piece of linen at least 5inches (13cm) larger than your completed dimension, hem the raw edges, fold in four and mark the folds with lines of tacking (basting) stitches.

2 Referring to the colour photograph for guidance, stitch a line of back stitch 2½inches (6.5cm) from the left-hand long edge, using two strands of stranded cotton (floss). Continue this line across the bottom, 2½inches (6.5cm) above the raw edge.

3 Lay the fabric on a clean, flat surface and, using a tape measure, mark the stitched line as follows.

4 Placing the tape along the line of stitching, place a pin at 4inch (10cm) intervals. Work a horizontal line using three back stitches to mark the position of the numbers (see diagram).

5 It is now possible to stitch the numbers as illustrated in the photograph and on the chart, checking that each digit is centred as you stitch.

6 Using the chart, add the air balloons in any combination you like, varying the colours and angles to suit the design. The example in the photograph was worked in three strands of stranded cotton (floss) for the cross stitch and two for all the back stitch outlining.

7 Make up the height chart as described in Materials and General Techniques on page 131.

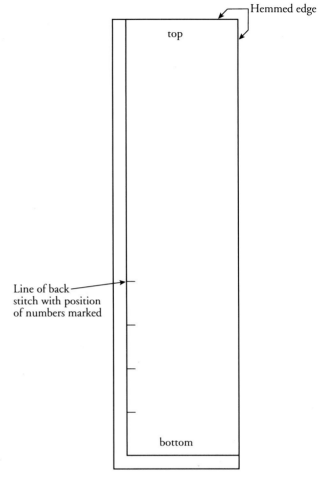

Marking the position of the numbers

8 To hang the project, it is a good idea to press gang some help! Ask your partner or a friend to hold the hanging against the wall and this will enable you to measure up from the floor until the stitched figures are at the right height. Mark the wall carefully and hang.

ANIMAL PLAY MAT

This project (see page 83) can be stitched quickly and makes an ideal gift for expectant mums and dads. The example in the photograph is stitched on an afghan shawl fabric with a soft pink and blue line included in the weave.

1 Referring to the charts on pages 84-5, stitch on a fabric with 14 threads per inch (2.5cm) and work over two threads, using all six strands. Stitch each motif within one of the squares and repeat the ball four times around the central section.

2 After the cross stitch is completed, you may add as much back stitch outline as you prefer. The animals in the photograph were outlined using two strands of stranded cotton (floss).

3 The edge of the play mat may be frayed as above.

80

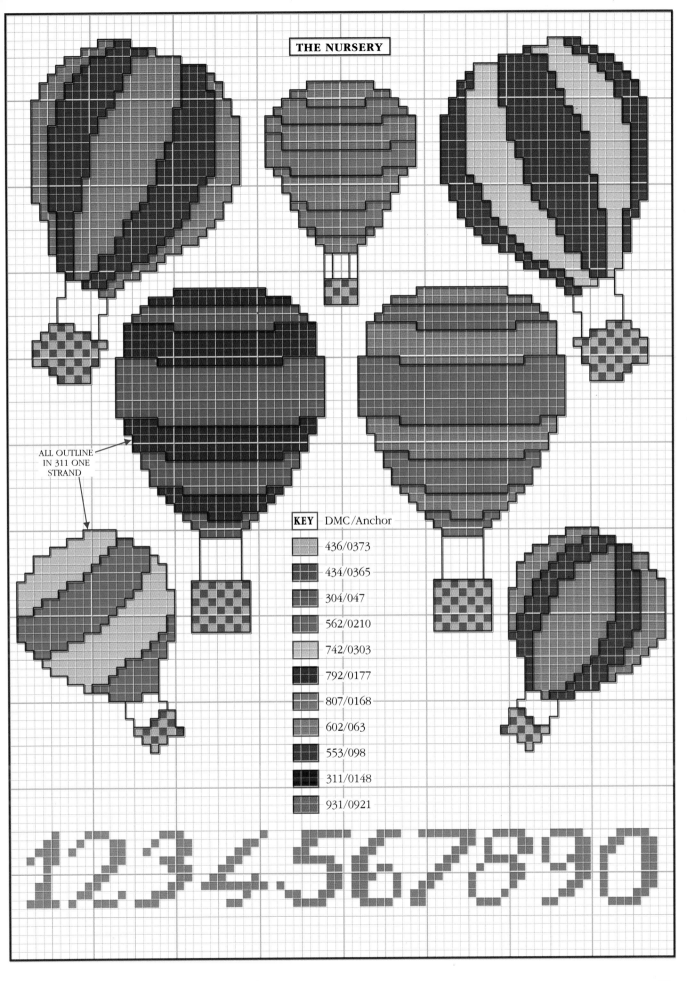

ALL OUTLINE
IN 311 ONE
STRAND

KEY	DMC/Anchor
	436/0373
	434/0365
	304/047
	562/0210
	742/0303
	792/0177
	807/0168
	602/063
	553/098
	311/0148
	931/0921

FIRST ANIMAL BOOK

I can remember the pleasure my babies showed when they were given rag books to look at and to chew. This simple project could be stitched by a brother or sister to give to a new baby. All the motifs are taken from the play mat, and these could include air balloons and alphabets, if desired.

Blue Aida, 11 blocks per inch (2.5cm)
Patterned fabric to make the spine and ribbon tie
Stranded cottons (floss), as listed on the chart on pages 84-5

1 Cut six pieces of Aida fabric at least 6inches (15cm) square. Each page of the book is made as follows.
2 Take one piece of fabric, work a narrow hem to prevent fraying. Fold in four and press lightly. Mark the folds with lines of tacking (basting) stitches to find the centre.

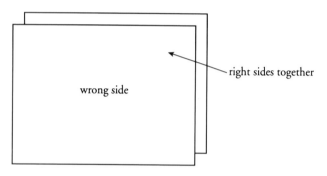

right sides together

wrong side

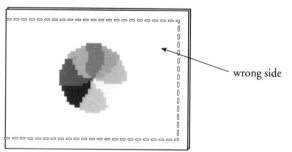

wrong side

Stitch around three sides

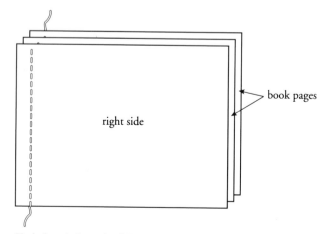

book pages

right side

Tack (baste) through all layers on unfinished edge

3 Choose the animal from the charts and find the central stitch before you begin stitching. I used three strands of stranded cotton (floss) for the cross stitch and two strands for the outlining.
4 Work each section in the same way, checking for missed stitches and pressing on the wrong side when completed.
5 Lay one of the stitched sections on a clean flat surface, wrong side down. Cover this with another stitched piece, so that right sides are together, matching raw edges. Pin in position. Stitch around three sides (see diagram), leaving a ⅝inch (2cm) seam allowance. Oversew the raw edges and then turn

right side out. Press lightly and set aside.

6 Make all remaining pages in the same manner.

7 Cut a strip of the patterned fabric for the spine 6inches (15cm) long and 2½inches (6.5cm) wide. Fold in half along the long edge and press.

8 Place all the 'pages' together, matching the finished edges and tack along the unfinished edge (see diagram). Place the strip of fabric over the raw edges, fold in a narrow hem and pin carefully. Stitch through all layers with matching thread, tucking in the raw edges as you stitch.

9 Cut another piece of the patterned fabric to make a pretty

Animal Play Mat and First Animal Book

tie. Cut the fabric 2½inches (6.5cm) wide and 20inches (50cm) long.

10 Fold in half along the long edge, tucking in the raw edges and pinning in position. Stitch along this edge with a sewing machine or by hand, using matching thread.

11 Neaten the ends and press with a hot iron. Thread through the book and tie in a bow. The bow is for decoration only and should be removed before a baby plays with it.

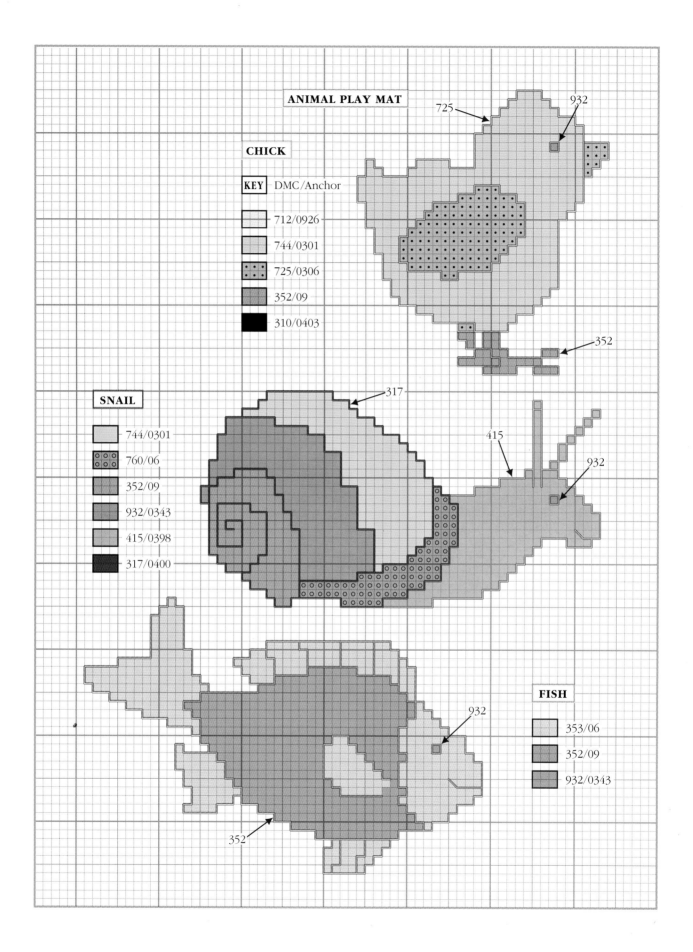

ANIMAL PLAY MAT

CHICK

KEY	DMC/Anchor
	712/0926
	744/0301
	725/0306
	352/09
	310/0403

725   932

352

SNAIL

	744/0301
	760/06
	352/09
	932/0343
	415/0398
	317/0400

317   415   932

FISH

	353/06
	352/09
	932/0343

932

352

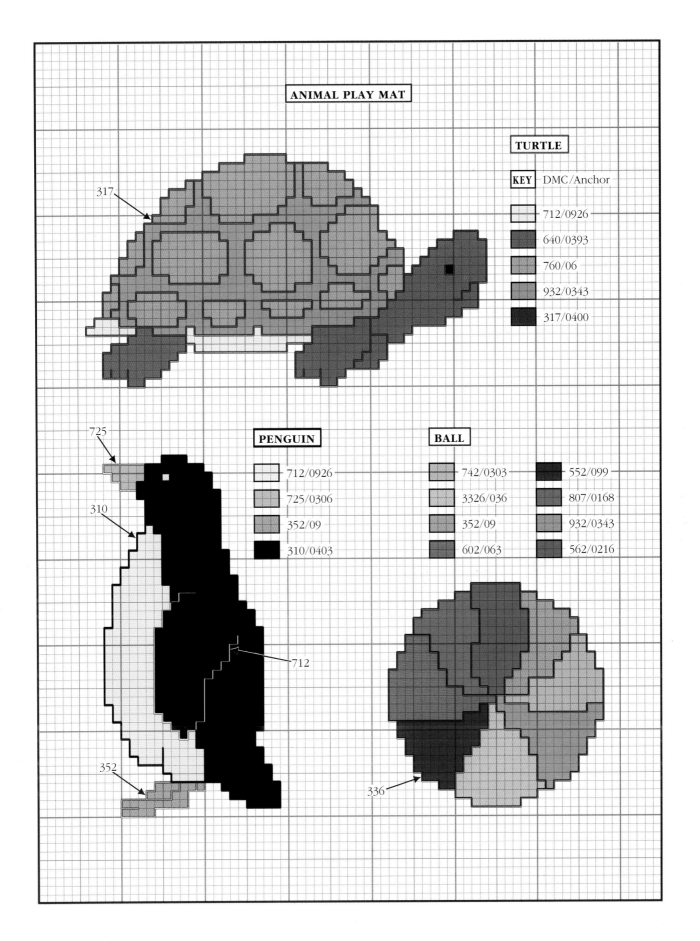

ANIMAL PLAY MAT

TURTLE

KEY	DMC/Anchor
	712/0926
	640/0393
	760/06
	932/0343
	317/0400

317

PENGUIN

	712/0926
	725/0306
	352/09
	310/0403

725

310

712

352

BALL

	742/0303		552/099
	3326/036		807/0168
	352/09		932/0343
	602/063		562/0216

336

9

THE
DEN

THE DEN

The den or study is probably a luxury concept for most of us - we do not have space to leave in situ unfinished stitching or a chess game. Meal times and family life will take precedence over hobbies. If you do not have a den, perhaps you could make a personal corner for the projects in this chapter.

GAMES SAMPLER

This design is the basis for two projects - a sampler and games box (see previous page). The sampler has extra motifs on the four corners, and the background around each number has been completed with cross stitch.

Design size: 11 x 9½inches (28 x 24cm)
Stitch count: 150 x 130

16 x 14½inches (40 x 36.5cm) cream Linda fabric, 27 threads per inch (2.5cm)
Stranded cottons (floss), as listed on the chart

1 Fold the Linda fabric in four and mark the fold lines with tacking (basting) stitches. Sew a narrow hem around the edge to prevent fraying.
2 Working from the centre of the chart, use two strands of stranded cotton (floss) for the cross stitch over two threads of the Linda fabric.
3 The back stitch outline is added after the cross stitch is complete, using one strand only.
4 Use one strand of black for the chess board, chess pieces, snake, border and draught board, and one strand of black to add French knots to the dice. One strand of black should be used for the running stitches or French knots on the crib board. Use one strand of white to add French knots to the dominoes. Work letters in two strands of blue, and noughts and crosses and hangman in two strands of green.
5 Mount and frame as described in Materials and General Techniques, page 130.

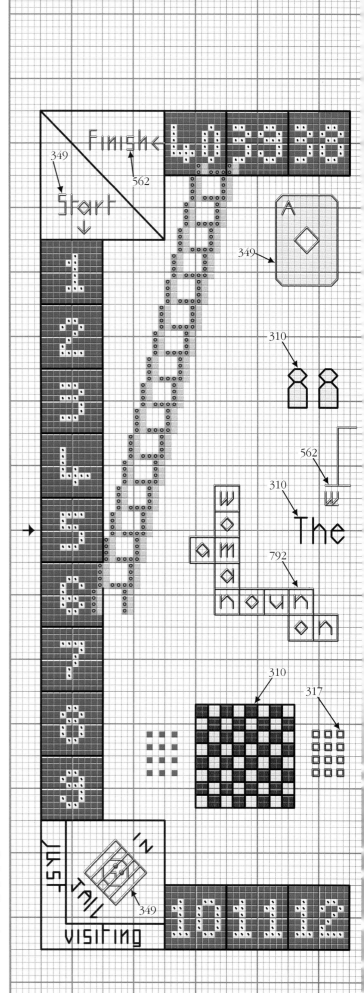

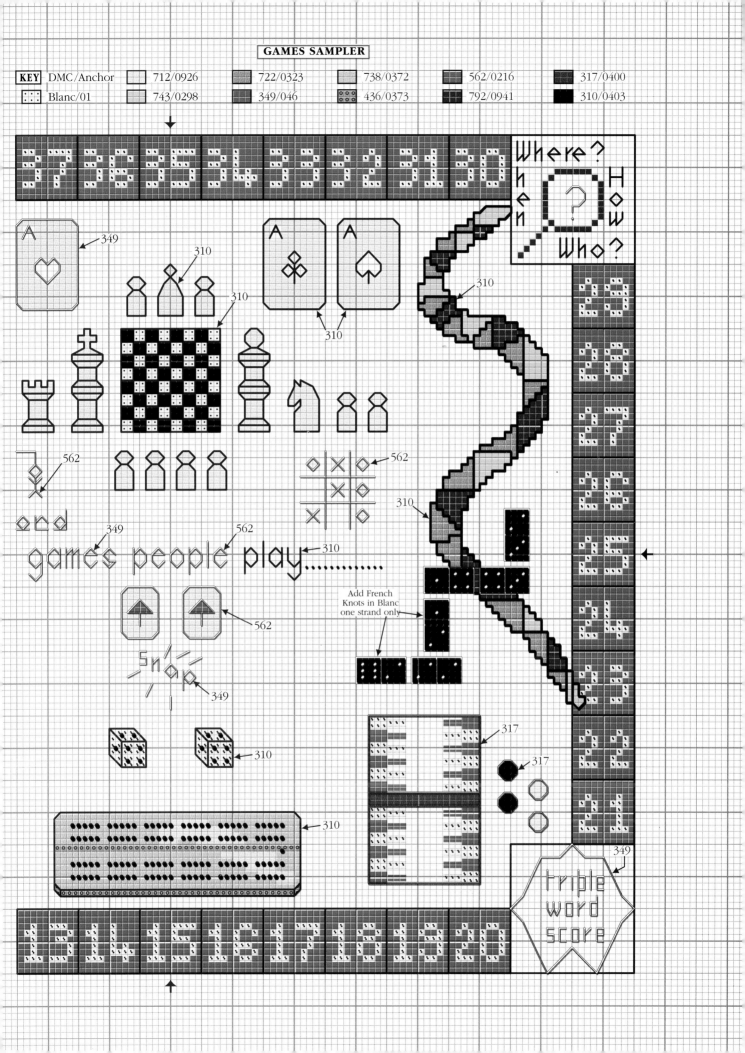

GAMES SAMPLER

GAMES BOX

This useful project uses the same chart as the Games Sampler but omits the corner motifs and uses a simple border of numerals within a back stitch outline. When using a purchased box for this project, check that the design will fit the aperture before you start stitching.

Design size: 8inches (20.5cm) square
Stitch count: 112 x 112

12 inches (30.5cm) square parchment Aida, 14 blocks per inch (2.5cm)
Stranded cottons (floss), as listed on the chart on pages 88-9
Purchased wooden box

1 Fold the Aida fabric in four and mark the folds with lines of tacking (basting) stitches. Sew a narrow hem around the edges to prevent fraying, and set aside.
2 Refer to Planning Your Own Designs on page 127 and carefully draw the box shapes for the numerals. Select the motifs you wish to include from the chart and add the outline to your drawing.
3 Stitch the design from the centre following the instructions for the Games Sampler, working the cross stitch over one block of Aida. Use two strands of stranded cotton (floss) for the cross stitch and one for the outline.
4 When the stitching is complete, make up following the manufacturer's instructions.

FLYING

This wonderful project was inspired by a particular occasion – my fortieth-birthday lunch over the Bay of Biscay on Concorde. A special gift from my husband!

Before starting this project, refer to Planning Your Own Designs on page 127. You will need to select the motifs you wish to include and draw the design on to graph paper. The border of kites can be varied to suit your design, or excluded if preferred.

The dimensions, measurements and instructions below refer to my version in the colour photograph.

Design size: 15¾ x 11inches (40 x 28cm)
Stitch count: 212 x 148

Blue Linda fabric, 27 threads per inch (2.5cm)
Stranded cottons (floss), as listed on the chart on pages 92-3

1 Cut a piece of fabric at least 5inches (3cm) larger than your completed dimensions.
2 I worked all the cross stitch using two strands of stranded cotton (floss), with one strand for the back stitch outline. All the kites and their tails were outlined using one strand of dark blue (shade DMC 792) in back stitch.
3 A line of bright red back stitch was stitched along Concorde's fuselage under the blue cross stitch, using two strands of stranded cotton (floss).

4 All remaining outlines were stitched in back stitch using one strand of the colour indicated on the chart.
5 Mount and frame as described in Materials and General Techniques, pages 128-9 and 130.

Flying and Spitfire Notebook

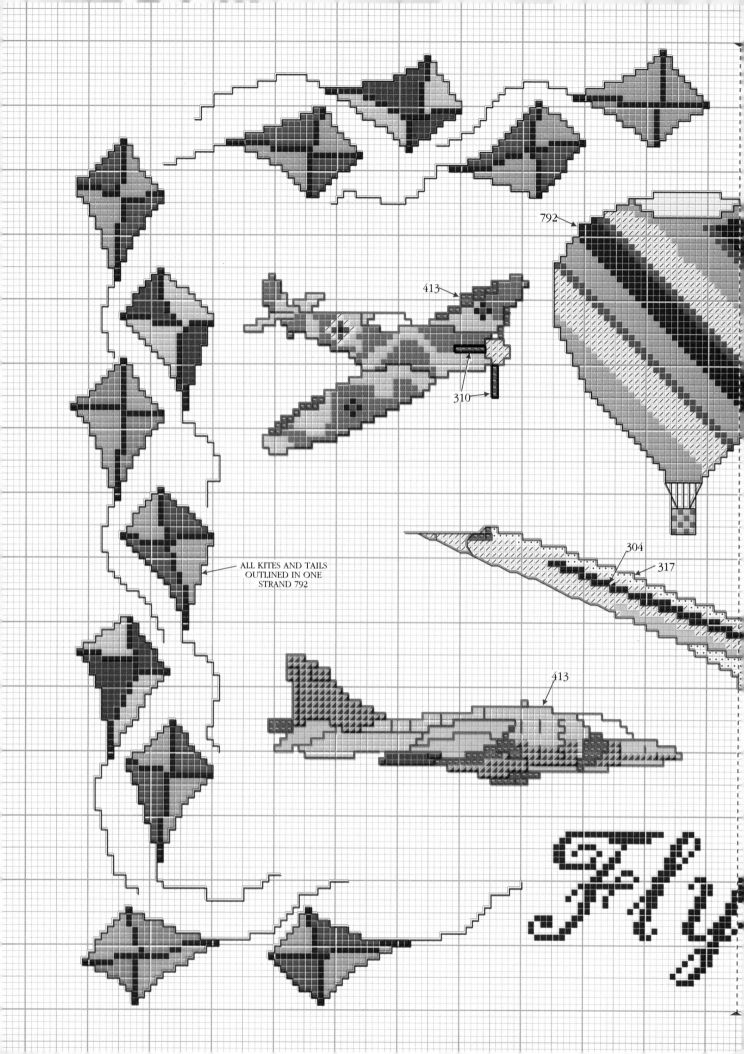

792

413

310

792

304

317

413

ALL KITES AND TAILS
OUTLINED IN ONE
STRAND 792

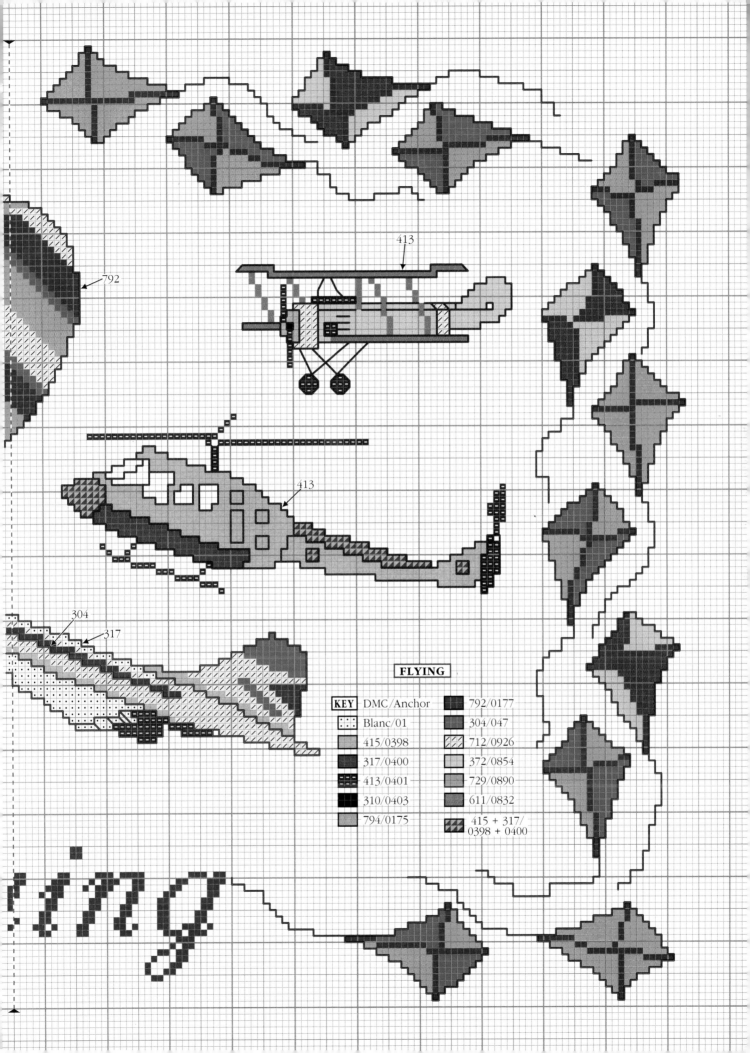

FLYING

KEY	DMC/Anchor		
	Blanc/01		792/0177
	415/0398		304/047
	317/0400		712/0926
	413/0401		372/0854
	310/0403		729/0890
	794/0175		611/0832
			415 + 317/ 0398 + 0400

433

898

310

433

413

413

413

317

433

317

310

433

BOATS AND BOATING

433

898

310

601

433

433

413

317

413

433

433

722/0323	601/077	926/0850	317/0400
605/050	807/0168	318/0399	413/0401

SPITFIRE NOTEBOOK

This design has been used to cover a purchased notebook, making a useful gift. If preferred, the book could be made as explained in Materials and General Techniques.

Rustic Aida, 14 blocks per inch (2.5cm)
Stranded cottons (floss), as listed on the chart on pages 92-3

1 Cut a piece of Aida fabric at least 7inches (18cm) wide and 4inches (10cm) long. Hem the raw edges and fold in four.
2 Work the Spitfire from the chart, using two strands of stranded cotton (floss) for the cross stitch and one for the back stitch outline.
3 When complete, check for missed stitches and press on the wrong side. Stretch and mount on a piece of self-adhesive mounting board (see Suppliers) and add the purchased note-book.

BOATS AND BOATING

This design (see previous page) began as a present for my father who, as a Trinity House pilot, spent all his working life on various types of ship. This project is not intended for the complete beginner, because it is necessary to plan the position of the boats and the rope border (see Planning Your Own Designs on page 127). The section of the border illustrated can be reversed and turned upside down to fit the design. The anchors included in the side borders are reversible and the ship's wheels are identical.
The design size and the stitch count refer to the design in the colour photograph.

Design size: 15 x 10inches (38 x 25.5cm)
Stitch count: 214 x 142

20 x 15inches (50 x 38cm) antique blue linen, 28 threads per inch (2.5cm)
Stranded cottons (floss), as listed on the chart on pages 94-5

1 Work a narrow hem around the edges of the linen to prevent fraying. Fold in four, press lightly and mark the folds with tacking (basting) stitches.
2 Look at the chart. Starting in the centre of the fabric and following the chart, work the sailing ship, using two strands of stranded cotton (floss) for the cross stitch and one strand for the back stitch outline.
3 When the large sailing boat is complete, count to the ship's wheel in the bottom centre and work the rope border from this point.
4 With the main vessel stitched and the border finished, you can decide how you want to arrange the remaining boats within the border.
5 When the design is complete, press lightly and frame as desired (see Materials and General Techniques, pages 127 and 130).

PINK SAILING BOAT FRAME

A perfect frame for the photographs of my two children, windblown at the top of the Worcester Beacon. The design size below refers to the worked example in the photograph on the previous page. The size will vary depending on the size of your photograph. You may need to adapt my instructions to suit.

Design size: 3inches (7.5cm) square
Stitch count: 41 x 41
Completed frame size: 9½ x 7½inches (24 x 19cm)

Dark-blue Aida, 14 blocks per inch (2.5cm)
Stranded cottons (floss), as listed on the chart on pages 94-5
Piece of stiff card
Craft knife
Rubber-based adhesive
Double-sided sticky tape

1 Cut a piece of Aida fabric at least 3inches (7.5cm) larger than the intended completed frame size, allowing for turnings.
2 Plan the position of the design, allowing for the opening for the picture.
3 Work the cross stitch from the chart, using two strands of stranded cotton (floss) for the cross stitch and one strand for the back stitch outline.
4 When the stitching is complete, press on the wrong side and set aside.
5 To make up the picture frame as illustrated in the photograph, refer to Materials and General Techniques, see pages 123-4 and 130.

FISHING SAMPLER

This interesting design (overleaf) evolved from a note-book kept by a fisherman friend as a record of 'the one that got away'. The design was based on some of his sketches, using freshwater fishing manuals for reference. All the fish are river varieties, but you could use some of the sea fish included in the Bathroom chapter.

All the designs in the photograph were stitched from the charts on pages 102-3. Before starting please refer to Planning Your Own Designs on page 127.

The dimensions and stitch count below refer to my version in the colour photograph. If you use another layout and/or fabric, your finished size will be different.

Design size: 10½ x 11inches (26.5 x 28cm)
Stitch count: 131 x 140

15½ x 16inches (39 x 40cm) pale-green linen, 25 threads per inch (2.5cm)
Stranded cottons (floss), as listed on the chart on pages 102-3

1 Work a narrow hem around the edges of the linen to prevent fraying. Fold in four and press lightly. Mark the folds with lines of tacking (basting) stitches.
2 This design may be stitched working from the bottom right-hand corner and not from the centre as is usually the case.
3 Look at the chart and, starting at point A, place your first stitch (dark green) 2½inches (6.5cm) diagonally from the bottom right-hand corner of the fabric.
4 Work the greenery, satchel, fishing rod, landing net and dead fish from the chart, using two strands of stranded cotton (floss).
5 Work the netting, fishing line and outline of the dead fish in back stitch, using one strand of stranded cotton (floss) in the shade indicated on the chart. Outline the leather satchel in two strands of dark brown, adding the French knots in black.
6 Looking at the colour photograph, plan the position of each fish. If you are a little nervous, draw each fish on a sheet of graph paper before you start.
7 Outline each fish in back stitch in the colour indicated on the chart, using one strand of stranded cotton (floss).
8 Referring to the colour photograph again, add the fishes' names in back stitch in one strand of dark blue.
9 When stitching is complete, press lightly on the wrong side and frame as desired (see Materials and General Techniques, pages 127 and 130).

FISHERMAN'S LOG BOOK

This useful little notebook (overleaf) is an ideal present for a fisherman friend. All the motifs you need are included in the Fishing Sampler, with the alphabet at the top of the chart.

The design may be adapted to suit a purchased notebook, or made up as described on page 129. If you intend to make a book cover, refer to the making up section in Materials and General Techniques at the back of the book for any additional requirements.

1 Plan the layout of the words and fish motifs on graph paper before you start stitching (refer to Planning Your Own Designs, page 127).
2 The example in the photograph was stitched on parchment Aida, 14 blocks per inch (2.5cm) using two strands of stranded cotton (floss) for the cross stitch and one for the back stitch outline.
3 When the stitching is complete, press lightly on the wrong side and make up as described in Materials and General Techniques. Add twisted cord to the book spine if preferred.

GONE FISHING PICNIC BAG

This fun project (overleaf) was stitched in coarse, unbleached linen using stranded cottons (floss). When complete, a lining of unbleached calico was added. If DMC stranded cottons (floss) are used, the picnic bag will be washable.

The dimensions below refer to my version in the colour photograph.

Overall bag size: 15 x 18inches (38 x 46cm)

Lamont unbleached linen, 20 threads per inch (2.5cm)
Stranded cottons (floss), as listed on the chart on pages 102-3
Lining fabric (optional)

1 Cut a piece of linen at least 5inches (13cm) larger than the completed project. Choose which fish you want to include and, using graph paper, as described in Planning Your Own Designs, page 127, map out the writing, the fish, and the rod and satchel motif.
2 I used three strands of stranded cotton (floss) for the cross stitch and two for the back stitch outline on the fish, the landing net and the fishing line.
3 Make up as described in Materials and General Techniques.

Overleaf:
Fishing Sampler, Fisherman's Logbook and Gone Fishing Picnic Bag

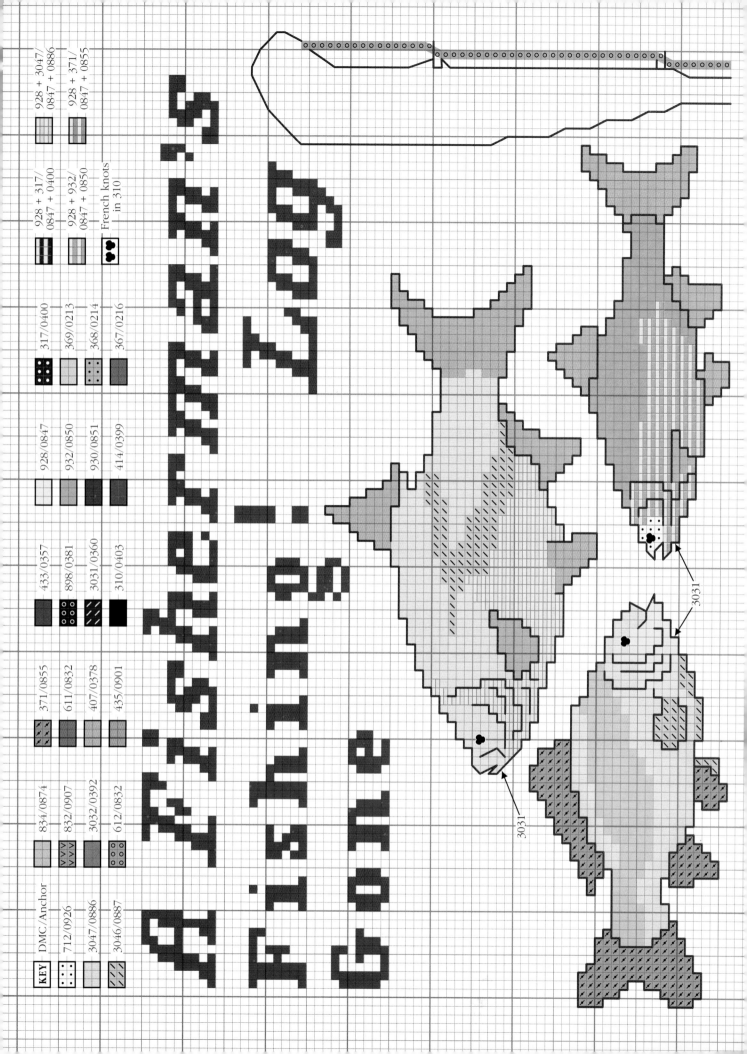

Perch Roach Pike Barbell

Common Carp Chubb

Bream Tench

Perch

3031

3031

3031

3031

3031

3031

898

FRENCH
KNOTS
IN 310

FISHING

ALL WRITING IN 930
ONE STRAND ONLY

A

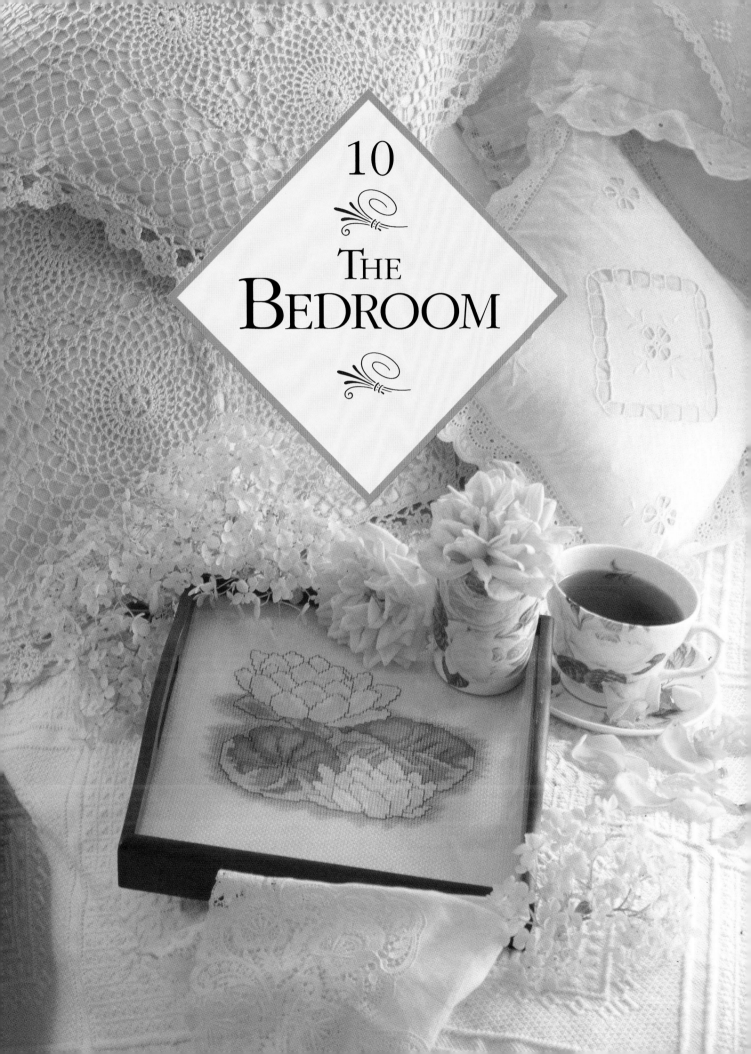

10

THE
BEDROOM

THE
BEDROOM

I have looked at pictures in magazines and wished for a frothy romantic bedroom with dozens of white lace cushions adorning a large brass bedstead. In reality, our bed is more likely to be adorned by our old tabby cat, a one-legged Cindy doll and copies of the Cricketer *magazine. There is also one item of furniture I am very attached to - a funny little 1930s nursing chair. Both my babies were nursed on it, as was their father before them. (see previous page).*

The water-lily design was made for that special bedroom chair, but will adapt to any chair, seat or footstool. Centre the large lily motif on the chair seat and add the smaller lily patterns to suit the size and shape of the chair.

The water-lilies are also shown stitched on cream damask Aida and placed in a pretty wooden tray.

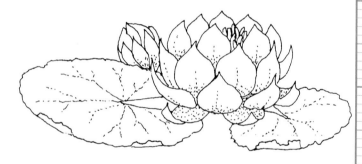

WATER-LILY
CHAIR SEAT

The instructions which follow are for a padded seat 14½ inches (36.5cm) square and a padded panel on the chair back 14½ x 11inches (36.5 x 28cm).

Design size: 13inches (33cm) square
Stitch count: 125 x 125 (not including random long stitch)

20inches (50cm) square Lamont Irish unbleached linen, 20 threads per inch (2.5cm)
Stranded cottons (floss), as listed on the chart

1 Work a narrow hem around the edges of the linen to prevent fraying. Fold in four, press lightly and mark the folds by working a line of tacking (basting) stitches.

Water-Lilies Seat and Tray

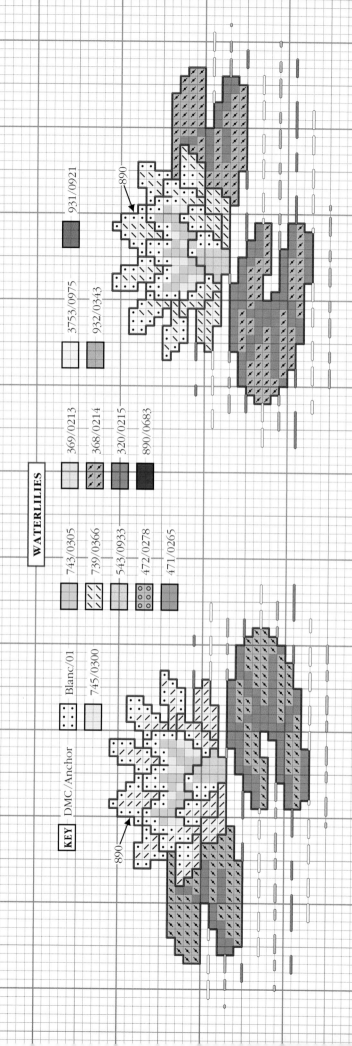

2 Following the chart and, starting in the centre, work the cross stitch using three strands of stranded cotton (floss) and stitching over two threads of linen.

3 For the back stitch outline on the lilies and the lily pads, one strand of stranded cotton (floss) may be sufficient, but if you prefer a stronger image, try using two strands.

4 After the cross stitch and the back stitch are completed, the water may be added. Using the chart as a guide only, work a series of random long stitches over anything from two to five threads on the linen. I have suggested the three shades of blue that were used on the original, but you may prefer to use more variety and incorporate threads you already have.

5 When the cross stitch is complete and you are satisfied with the water, check for missed stitches, press on the wrong side, and set aside.

WATER-LILY CHAIR BACK PANEL

The back panel on the chair has been worked by repeating a single small lily motif in the four corners of the fabric. For this reason, the design size and stitch count below refer to one lily motif only. In each case, the random long stitches for the water are not included.

Design size: 4 x 2½ inches (10 x 6.5cm)
Stitch count: 39 x 24 (individual lily motif)

18½ x 15inches (47 x 38cm) Lamont Irish unbleached linen, 20 threads per inch (2.5cm)
Stranded cottons (floss) as above

1 Prepare the linen as for the chair seat.

2 Stitch individual lily motifs from the chart repeating outline colours and long stitch for the water.

3 When the stitching is complete, press on the wrong side and set aside.

4 The nursing chair in the photograph already had a wooden seat and back panel, so I made a simple padded cushion with a solid base for the seat and back sections (see Materials and General Techniques page 132).

WATER-LILY TRAY

There is a large selection of manufactured trays available from good needlework shops. Before stitching, choose the motif you wish to reproduce and check the stitch count to ensure the design will fit your tray.

The design in the photograph on pages 104–5 was stitched on Damask Aida, using two strands of stranded cotton (floss) for the cross stitch and one for the back stitch outline. I have used dark green to outline the lily petals to give more definition to the tray.

WILD ROSE JEWELLERY ROLL

This delicate but useful wild rose project was inspired by the mass of tiny pink and peach roses covering the hedgerows near our cottage. The design is stitched on ivory linen, but would look equally effective on a black or navy blue background. The project uses a simple strip of fabric, which is then stitched, bound and rolled (see page 132).

Design size: 4½ x 5½ inches (11.5 x 14cm)
Stitch count: 65 x 81

28 x 9inches (71 x 23cm) ivory linen, 28 threads per inch (2.5cm)
Stranded cottons (floss), as listed on the chart on page 111
Polyester wadding
Lining fabric
Satin ribbon

1 Work a narrow hem around the edges of the linen to prevent fraying. Fold the linen in half, bringing the two short edges together. Crease along the fold. Fold again in the same direction, creasing along the second fold to create four equal sections. Mark the fold with tacking (basting) stitches. The design is stitched in one of the end sections.

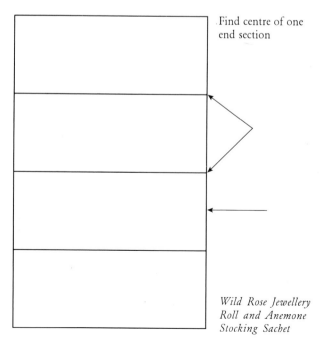

Find centre of one end section

Wild Rose Jewellery Roll and Anemone Stocking Sachet

2 Find the centre of one end section (see diagram) and work the design from the chart, using two strands of stranded cotton (floss) for the cross stitch and one strand for the back stitch outlining.

3 When the cross stitch is complete, select the yellow shades and work random French knots (see More Advanced Stitches

on page 126), on top of the cross stitch to form the flower centres.

4 When the stitching is complete, press on the wrong side and make up as described in Materials and General Techniques on pages 127 and 132.

ANEMONE STOCKING SACHET

This 'frothy' project is perfect for those special expensive stockings that you cannot really afford to wear!

Design size: 7 x 4inches (18 x 10 cm)
Stitch count: 99 x 55

12 x 8inches (30.5 x 20.5cm) dusty pink linen, 28 threads per inch (2.5cm)
Stranded cottons (floss), as listed on the chart
Cotton lace in antique white (optional)
Silk lining fabric
Polyester wadding
Matching satin binding

1 Sew a narrow hem all round the linen to prevent fraying
2 Lay the linen on a clean flat surface with the short edge towards you. Fold the linen into three 4inch (10cm) sections and mark the folds with lines of tacking (basting) stitches.

3 Centre the design in the bottom section of the fabric, working the cross stitch in two strands of stranded cotton (floss) and the outline and the flower stalks in one strand, as indicated on the chart.

4 When the cross stitch is complete, check for missed stitches and press lightly on the wrong side.

5 See Materials and General Techniques, pages 131-2, to complete.

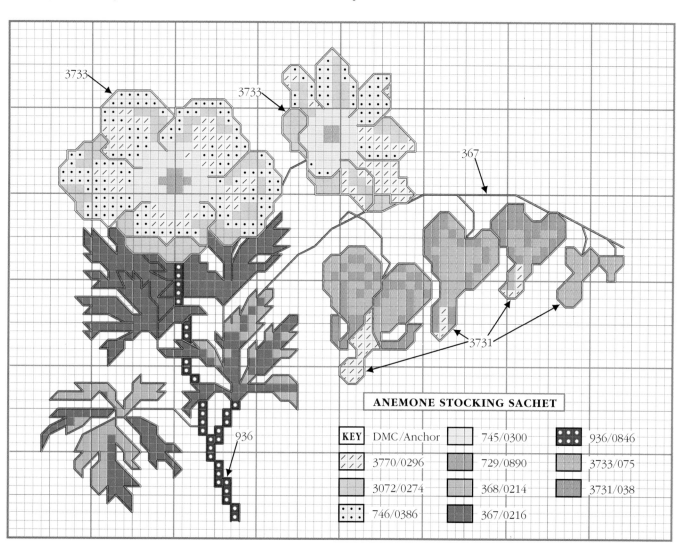

ANEMONE STOCKING SACHET			
KEY DMC/Anchor		745/0300	936/0846
3770/0296		729/0890	3733/075
3072/0274		368/0214	3731/038
746/0386		367/0216	

WILD ROSE JEWELLERY ROLL

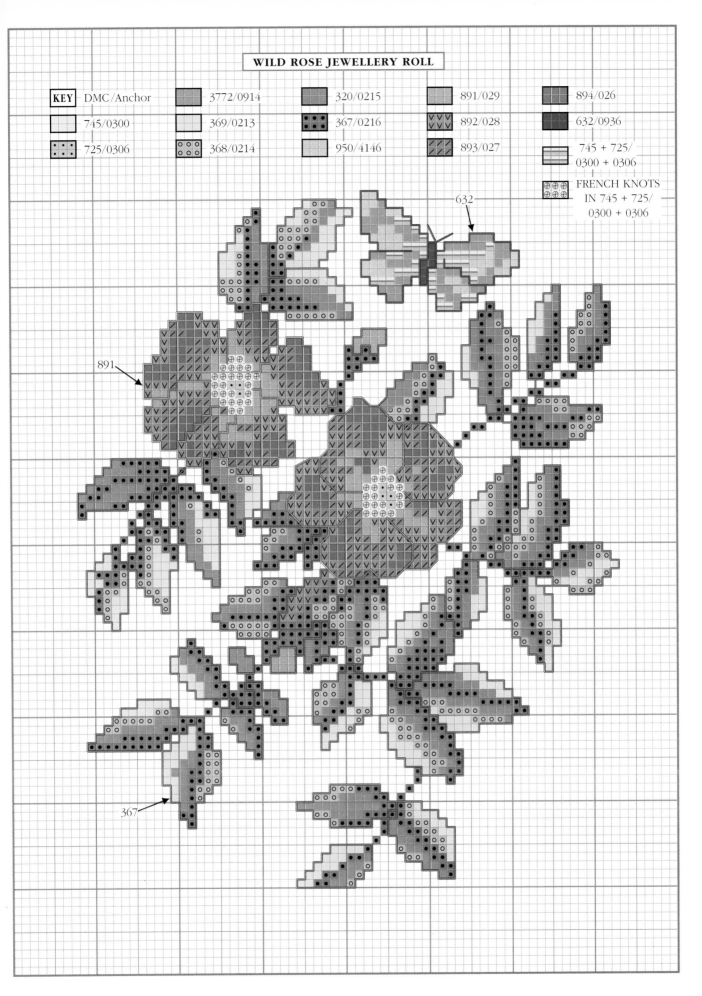

KEY DMC/Anchor · 3772/0914 · 320/0215 · 891/029 · 894/026
745/0300 · 369/0213 · 367/0216 · 892/028 · 632/0936
725/0306 · 368/0214 · 950/4146 · 893/027 · 745 + 725/ 0300 + 0306
FRENCH KNOTS IN 745 + 725/ 0300 + 0306

632

891

367

11
CHRISTMAS
AT HOME

CHRISTMAS AT HOME

*For many years I spent my Christmas Day working in a busy hospital ward,
and it has taken some time to adjust to the family occasion. These days, Christmas
at home means a big tree, a log fire and early morning tiptoes to see if
Father Christmas has been.
The charts in this chapter include a number of seasonal motifs for you to use
as you please. If using a motif to fill a card, check the stitch count of the individual
motif to ensure it will fit.*

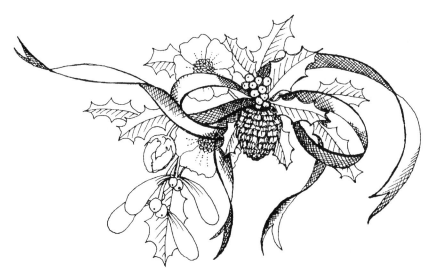

ADVENT RING

This idea (see previous page) came from Germany, where four candles are fixed to the ring and are lit during December. You will need to decide where the Advent Ring will hang and adjust the length of the linen band to suit.

3 lengths of eyelet band 2inches (5cm) wide, 28 threads per inch (2.5cm)
6 lengths of narrow ribbon if desired
Stranded cottons (floss), as listed on the charts on page 118
6 small brass rings

1 Decide on the length of the band and cut three pieces the same size.
2 Select the motifs you wish to include and position the stitching at regular intervals.
3 When the stitching is complete, press on the wrong side and finish as follows.
6 Add candle holders if desired.

CHURCH WINDOW CARD

This design (see previous page) can be adapted to suit other festivals by simply altering the colour scheme. If the reds are replaced with yellows and the design fitted into a white or cream card, it makes an ideal Easter card.

Design size: 2½ x 4½inches (6.5 x 11.5cm)
Stitch count: 34 x 58

4½ x 6inches (11.5 x 15cm) cream Aida, 14 blocks per inch (2.5cm)
Stranded cottons (floss), as listed on the charts on page 119
Red arched card

1 Fold the Aida fabric in four and press lightly.
2 Referring to the chart, work the design from the centre, using two strands of stranded cotton (floss) for the cross stitch and one strand for the outline, the window and the brickwork.
3 When the cross stitch is complete, check for missed stitches and press on the wrong side.
4 Make up as instructed in Materials and General Techniques on pages 129-30.

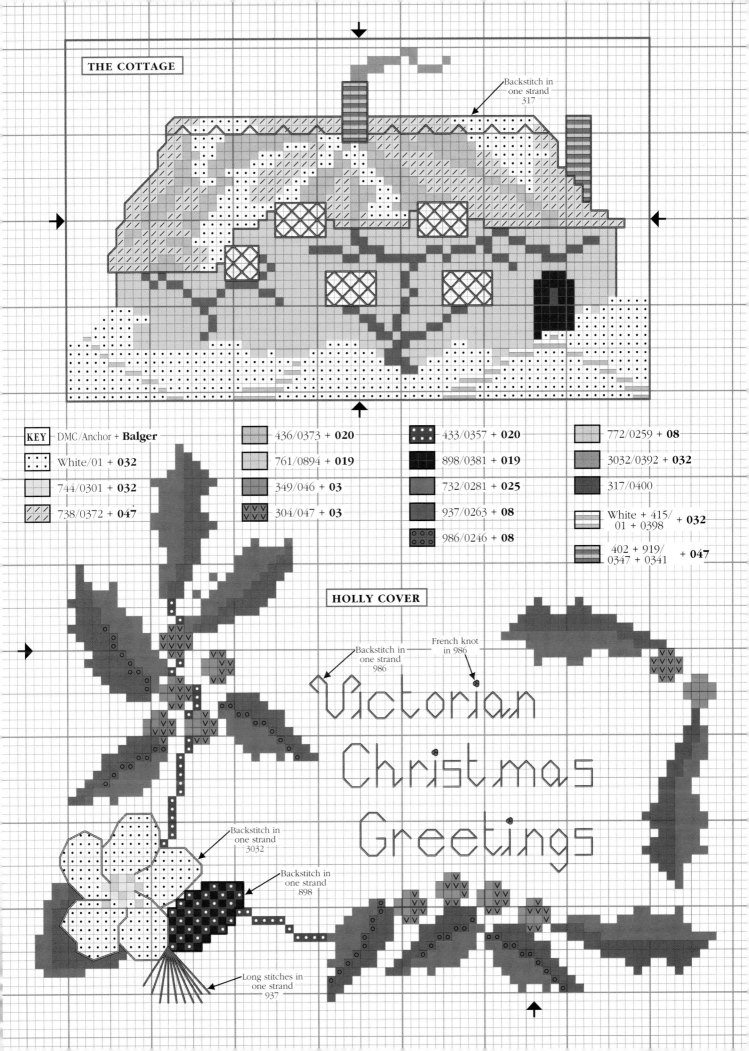

THE COTTAGE

Backstitch in
one strand
317

KEY	DMC/Anchor + **Balger**

White/01 + **032**

744/0301 + **032**

738/0372 + **047**

436/0373 + **020**

761/0894 + **019**

349/046 + **03**

304/047 + **03**

433/0357 + **020**

898/0381 + **019**

732/0281 + **025**

937/0263 + **08**

986/0246 + **08**

772/0259 + **08**

3032/0392 + **032**

317/0400

White + 415/
01 + 0398 + **032**

402 + 919/
0347 + 0341 + **047**

HOLLY COVER

Backstitch in
one strand
986

French knot
in 986

Victorian
Christmas
Greetings

Backstitch in
one strand
3032

Backstitch in
one strand
898

Long stitches in
one strand
937

CHRISTMAS MOTIFS AND BOOK COVER

The remaining designs in the charts on pages 118-19 can be used in cards, small frames to hang on the tree, gift tags, place settings and lots more.

The examples in the colour photograph on page 112 are worked on Aida or Linda fabrics, using two strands for the cross stitch and one for any outline necessary.

The Christmas book cover provides the perfect place to keep all those recipes, last year's cards, the present list and all those important Christmas reminders.

The design is made in two parts, but if preferred, all the design could be stitched in one piece. I worked the cottage on half-bleached linen and used white linen for the outer cover. The book cover measures 10½ x 7inches (26.5 x 18cm). To add a Christmassy sparkle to the design, I used Balger blending filament, combining its gossamer thread with the stranded cotton (floss) to give the design – especially the snow – a special glitter.

COTTAGE
Design size: 2¾ x 3⅞inches (7 x 9.8cm)
Stitch count: 41 x 70

HOLLY COVER
Design size: 8 x 5½inches (20.5 x 14cm)
Stitch count: 120 x 82

Half-bleached linen, 30 threads per inch (2.5cm)
White linen, 30 threads per inch (2.5cm)
Stranded cottons (floss), as listed on the chart on page 115
Balger blending filament, as listed on the chart

1 To stitch the cottage, cut a piece of linen at least 5inches (13cm) larger than the finished dimension. Fold in four, press lightly and mark the folds with a line of tacking (basting) stitches.
2 Looking at the cottage section of the chart, begin stitching the cottage from the centre. Use two strands of stranded cotton (floss) and two strands of blending filament for the cross stitch and one strand of stranded cotton (floss) for the back stitch outline.
3 When complete, check for missed stitches, press lightly and set aside.
4 To stitch the holly cover, cut two pieces of linen at least 5inches (13 cm) larger than the completed book cover, setting one aside. Fold in four, marking the folds with tacking (basting) stitches.
5 Looking at the holly section of the chart, count from the centre to the holly and berries on the left of the chart.
6 Following the instructions for the cottage section, complete the cross stitch, check for missed stitches and press lightly.
7 Make up as described in Materials and General Techniques on page 129.

Christmas Book

CHRISTMAS DECORATIONS

304

304

937

937

304

ADVENT RING

304

304

729

KEY	DMC/Anchor		729/0890		321/046		937/0268		Metallic gold
	743/0305		304/047		989/0242		792/0177		

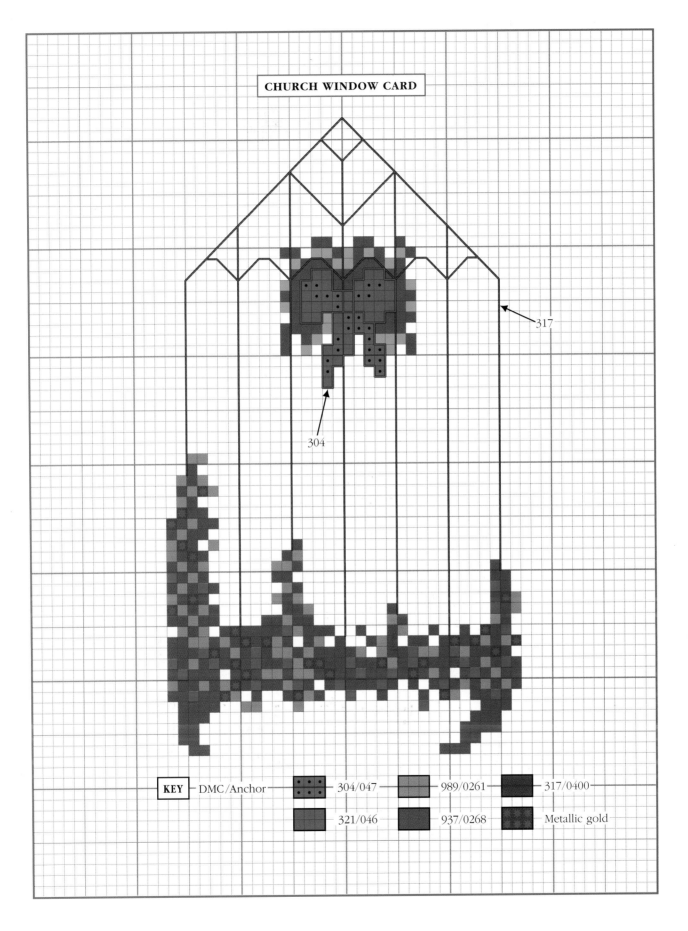

CHURCH WINDOW CARD

317

304

KEY	DMC/Anchor	304/047	989/0261	317/0400
		321/046	937/0268	Metallic gold

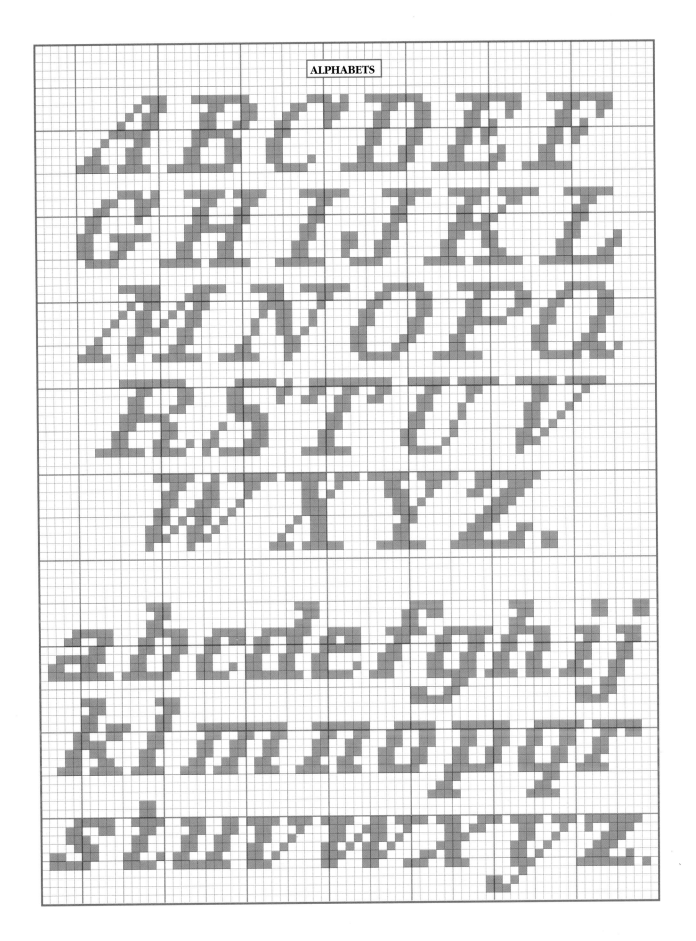

ALPHABETS

MATERIALS AND GENERAL TECHNIQUES

THE ESSENTIALS OF COUNTED CROSS STITCH

All the projects in this book are designed to be counted from a cross stitch chart. If you have never attempted counted cross stitch before, you might find it useful to stitch one of the smaller designs first, before tackling a larger project. Once mastered, the basic stitch is very simple. All the projects illustrated are based on cross stitch with additional stitches in a few cases.

To complete some of the larger items in the colour photographs, you will need to plan a layout and sometimes you will need to combine motifs from different charts. As you stitch, I am sure you will become your own most ardent critic and you will develop more specific skills, so I have included some special techniques that you might find useful when you reach that stage. First of all though, the basics!

All counted designs are made up of squares or parts of squares. The principle is that the picture, motif or pattern is transferred to the fabric by matching the weave of the fabric to the pattern or chart. The term 'counted' means that the design is transferred onto the fabric by counting the squares on the chart and matching this on the fabric, so that each stitch will be put in the right place.

FABRICS

The fabrics used for counted cross stitch are all even-weave fabrics, which means that they have the same number of threads or blocks per inch (2.5cm) in both directions. The warp and weft are woven evenly so that, when a stitch is formed, it will appear as a square or part of a square.

There are dozens of even-weave fabrics available for counted needlework, far too many to include here, so I will only mention the ones I like to use.

When choosing fabrics for counted cross stitch, the thread count is the method used by manufacturers to differentiate between the varieties available, so the higher the number or the more threads or stitches per inch (2.5cm), the finer the fabric.

AIDA

This excellent cotton fabric is specifically woven for counted needlework and is ideal for the beginner. The threads are woven in blocks rather than singly. There has been a tendency for linen snobs to avoid Aida, which I feel is such a pity. There are many projects that suit this fabric particularly well as it ensures an even and very square stitch, quite different to the finish on linen or similar fabrics. Aida is available in 8, 11, 14, 16 and 18 blocks per inch (2.5cm). If you require even finer fabric, it is possible to use Hardanger, which is 22 blocks per inch (2.5cm).

When stitching on Aida, one block on the fabric corresponds to one square on the chart. Working a cross stitch on Aida is exactly the same as on linen, except that, instead of counting threads, you count the single blocks. The only disadvantage with Aida is that, because there is no central hole

on the fabric, it is more difficult to work three-quarter stitches, so that linen or related materials would be preferable. This is explained in the next section and in the diagram on page 126.

LINEN

This lovely, if slightly more expensive, material is commonly used for counted cross stitch. Stitching on linen is no more complicated than stitching on Aida but it requires a different technique. Linen has irregularities in the fabric, which occur naturally and add charm to the finished piece, but to even out any discrepancies complete cross stitches are usually worked over two threads in each direction.

The choice of colour must depend on personal taste and the type of project in hand. Linen is generally available in white, 'old' white or ivory, cream and raw or unbleached shades. The projects in this book also include some of the wonderful new coloured linens.

It is quite easy to make a piece of white or ivory linen look old by dipping the washed fabric in cold tea. Simply make a pot of tea and leave it to brew in the usual way. Pour the tea into a clean bowl through a strainer and soak the linen, stirring occasionally, for about ten minutes. Drip-dry naturally and iron before stitching.

If you wish to 'age' an existing worked piece, this too can be dipped in tea, embroidery included! You must be sure that the thread used is colour-fast before you start but otherwise the procedure is the same.

LINEN BAND

There are a number of banded products on the market, both in Aida and in linen. The bands used in this book all come from Germany and are available in a variety of widths, styles and colours. They are made from pure linen, sometimes with decorative edges added in cotton.

ZWEIGART LINDA

This fabric, similar to linen in appearance but made from a mixture of cotton and synthetics, is ideal for products that need to be easy-care, such as baby and table linens.

AFGHAN FABRICS

These soft fabrics made from mixed fibres are produced for shawl-like projects which can look wonderful thrown over the back of a chair. They are usually sold in squares or pattern repeats.

STITCHING PAPER

Early Victorian stitched paper articles were often bookmarks of a religious nature, with verses or pieces of scripture worked in cross stitch or long stitch. During the nineteenth century, European ladies could take classes in cutting and stitching techniques and some very elaborate designs were produced. The Victorians were very fond of this medium. Some of the samplers seen in Victorian scenes were stitched on paper, with later examples including needle and card cases, table mats, lampshades and even handkerchief boxes.

Today's stitching paper is closely based on the punched card or paper used by the Victorians. It is now available in 14 holes per inch (2.5cm) and can be stitched, glued, sculpted and folded.

Stitching on paper is quite different to fabric, so here are some hints:
● Although the paper is quite strong, do remember to touch it carefully, because it will tear if roughly handled.
● There is a right and a wrong side to the paper, the smoother side being the right side.
● Avoid folding the paper unless this is part of the design. Find the centre with a ruler and mark with a pencil. The lines can be removed with a soft rubber.

THREADS

All the projects in this book have been stitched with DMC stranded cotton (floss). Stranded cotton is made up of six strands of mercerised cotton, usually divided before stitching. For all the projects in the colour photographs, I have indicated how many threads were used. All the designs could be stitched in Anchor cottons, but it is not possible to achieve a perfect colour match.

When you are stitching on linen and you are not sure of the number of strands needed for the cross stitch, the best way is to carefully pull out a thread of the fabric and compare this with your chosen yarn. The thread on your needle should be roughly the same weight as that of the fabric.

When selecting threads, always have the fabric you are intending to use at hand, because the colour of your background material will affect your choice of colours. When in a shop, check the colour of the thread in daylight as electric light can 'kill' some shades. It is possible now to buy daylight bulbs to use in normal spotlights at home – a great help when shading a design in the evening.

It really does pay to start with good habits if possible and have an organiser for your threads. There are many excellent organiser systems on the market, but I make my own organiser cards, as shown in the diagram. The card from inside a packet of tights is excellent, but any stiff card will do. Punch holes down each side and take a skein of stranded cotton. Cut the cotton into manageable lengths of about 20 inches (50cm) and thread them through the holes as shown. It is quite easy to remove one length of thread from the card without disturbing the rest. If you label the card with the manufacturer's name and shade number, when the project is complete, all the threads will be labelled ready for the next design.

Stranded cotton (floss) can be used in conjunction with Balger blending filament, which is a gossamer-thin yarn that will add lustre and sparkle to your design.

NEEDLES

With all counted needlework you will need blunt tapestry needles of various sizes, depending on which fabric you choose. The most commonly-used tapestry needles for cross stitch are sizes 24 and 26. Avoid leaving the needle in the material when it is put away as it may rust and mark the fabric. The nickel plating on ordinary needles varies so much that some stitchers find their needles mark and discolour very quickly. As a result they treat themselves to gold-plated needles, which can be used again and again.

If you are not sure which size needle to select, it is possible to check in the following way. Push the needle through the fabric. It should pass through without enlarging the hole but also without falling through without any pressure.

When beads are suggested on a chart you can use a beading needle, but as these tend to be very expensive, the beads can be attached using a fine, sharp needle and a half cross stitch.

FRAMES AND HOOPS

This subject always raises questions and argument. I never use a frame or hoop for counted cross stitch, but I always

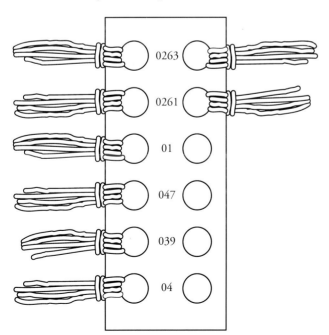

Make your own organiser

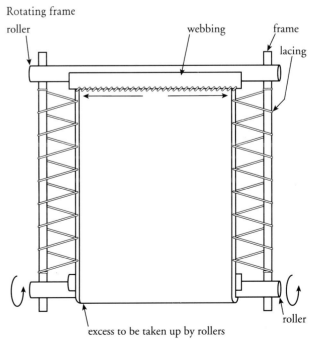

Rotating frame

roller   webbing   frame   lacing   excess to be taken up by rollers   roller

do when stitching on canvas. This is a personal choice and you must do what you like. If you feel more comfortable with a frame or hoop then use one. I prefer to cuddle my cross stitch as I work and a frame would get in the way!

If you decide to use a rectangular frame these come in a variety of shapes and sizes, some free-standing, some that clip on the arm of the chair to keep both hands free. The needlework is stitched to the webbing along the width of the frame with the excess fabric held on rollers at the top and bottom (see diagram).

If you use a hoop, ensure that all the design is within the

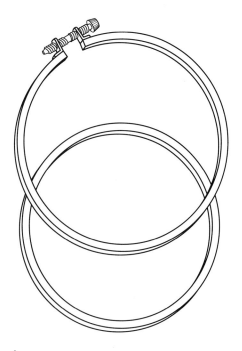

Wooden hoop

stitching area of the hoop and that you do not need to keep moving it, as this will drag and spoil the stitches. There are a variety of hoops in many sizes and styles so you should find something to suit you (see diagram).

SCISSORS

Keep a small, sharp pair of pointed scissors exclusively for your stitching. I wear mine around my neck on a piece of ribbon now, so that I don't have to spend time hunting for them down the sides of the sofa.

THE PRINCIPLE OF THE CHARTS

A needlework chart may be a series of symbols or coloured squares on paper, or a combination of both, as is the case with this book. Stitchers are very vocal about which sort of chart they prefer - this book hopes to please everyone by including both kinds.

The charts are designed on computer and are as clearly defined as possible, but we have also added symbols to the coloured squares to help differentiate between the shades.

Whichever chart you prefer to use, the principle is the same for either type. Each square, both occupied and unoccupied, represents two threads of linen or one block of Aida. Each occupied square equals one stitch. At this stage,

each stitch is presumed to be a complete cross stitch. When you look at the charts within the book, you will see that there are some part stitches, ie three-quarter stitches (see page 126). How to form three-quarter stitches is described later.

All that determines the size of a cross stitch design is the number of stitches up and down. If you are familiar with knitting, it is similar to the same number of stitches worked in 4-ply wool and in a chunky weight. To calculate the design size, look at the chart and count the number of stitches in each direction. Divide this number by the number of stitches per inch on the fabric of your choice and this will determine the completed design size.

The crucial factor with any counted needlework is the stitch count and the fabric count. Where relevant in the designs in this book I have given a stitch count and a dimension of the completed work, but remember this will only apply if you have used the same fabric. Remember also that you are counting the threads and not the spaces. You might find it useful to think of the linen as a ladder and count the rungs not the holes. Try not to travel between areas of colour, unless the thread can be hidden behind existing stitches.

Before starting a project, it is vital to check the thread count of your chosen fabric and the stitch count of the chart you are intending to use and make sure that the design will fit. This is particularly important when the finished piece needs to fit a special frame, trinket pot or card.

FIRST STITCHES

A cross stitch has two parts and can be worked in one of two ways. A complete stitch can be worked (see diagram), or a number of half stitches can be sewn in one line, then completed in a second journey (see diagram). The one essential rule is that all the top stitches face the same direction.

For this example the cross stitch is being worked on linen,

Single cross stitch showing needle position

over two threads of the fabric, using two strands of stranded cotton (floss). Bring the needle up through the wrong side at the bottom left, cross two fabric threads and insert at top right. Push the needle through, then bring it up at the bottom right-hand corner, ready to complete the stitch in the top left-hand corner. To work the adjacent stitch, bring the needle up at the bottom right-hand corner of the first stitch (thus the stitches share points of entry and exit). To make part-completed stitches, work the first leg of the cross stitch as above, but instead of completing the stitch, work the next half stitch and continue to the end of the row. The cross is completed on the return journey.

Having learnt the basic cross stitch, you now need to know how to start off, using the knotless loop start. This method can be very useful with stranded cotton, but it

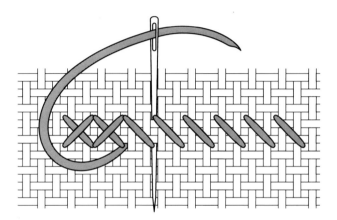

Part-completed stitches – completed on return journey

only works if you are intending to stitch with an even number of strands, ie 2, 4 or 6. Cut the stranded cotton roughly twice the length you would normally need and carefully separate one strand. Double this thread and thread your needle. Pierce your fabric from the wrong side where you intend to start your first stitch, leaving the looped end at the rear of the work (see diagram). Return your needle to the wrong side after forming a half cross stitch, and pass the needle through the waiting loop. Thus the

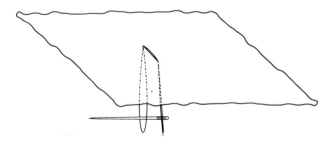

Knotless loop start

stitch is anchored and you can begin stitching. When stitching with an uneven number of strands, start by anchoring the thread at the back of the work under the first few stitches.

It can be nerve-wracking at the start, when you are faced with a plain, unprinted piece of fabric, but it is really very simple. The secret is to start in the middle of the fabric and in the middle of the chart, unless stated. Using this method, there will always be enough fabric to stretch and frame. It is always a good rule of thumb to cut your fabric

at least 5inches (13cm) larger than the intended completed dimension.

To find the middle of the fabric, fold it in four and press lightly. Open out and work a line of tacking (basting) stitches following the threads to mark the folds and the centre. These stitches are removed when the work is completed (see diagram). Check you have all the colours you need and mount all threads on a piece of card alongside its shade number. Sew a narrow hem or oversew the edges to prevent fraying. This can be removed on completion.

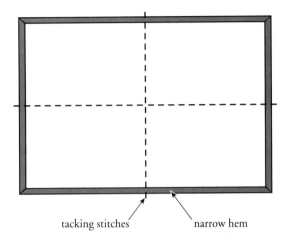

tacking stitches   narrow hem

Fold fabric in four and tack along folds

Thread your needle with the required number of threads and you are ready to go! Remember to work the design from the middle to ensure an adequate border for stretching and framing.

MORE ADVANCED STITCHES

Now that you have mastered the basic principles of counted cross stitch we can consider other techniques used to enhance the design.

Outlining is the addition of a back stitch outline to add detail or dimension to a picture (see diagram). In all the charts in this book, the solid lines surrounding the coloured squares refer to back stitch outline, with the colour indicated by the shade number on the chart. Outlining is an optional part of cross stitch. If you examine examples

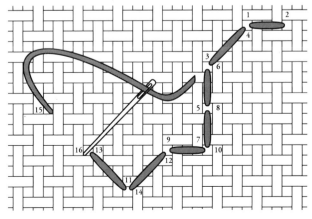

Back stitch

Three-quarter stitch

working a French knot finished knot

French knots

from the entry point. This stops the stitch pulling through to the wrong side. If you want to work bigger knots, add more thread to the needle – this seems to give a much better finish than winding more times.

Algerian Eye is a pretty, star-shaped stitch that may be added to cross stitch pictures with great effect. The stitch occupies the space taken by four cross stitches and is worked in such a way that a small hole is formed in the centre, which is part of its charm.

Random uncounted French knots are almost free embroidery without the panic and they are great fun. I outline an area with a single thread in back stitch and then pack in as many French knots as I like within the area. This can be very effective (see the dandelion below). This technique can be

of Danish counted cross stitch you will see that added outlining was comparatively rare. Sometimes it can be an excuse for a poor design which would not be clear without it. It is best to look at the completed cross stitch design first and then decide if it is necessary to add an outline. Always add the outlining after the cross stitch is complete.

You will recognise **three-quarter stitch** on the chart, as it will only occupy half a coloured square rather than one whole square. Work the first half of the stitch as described in First Stitches, but when the second part of the stitch is formed, the needle is pushed through the middle hole thus forming a triangular stitch (see diagram).

French knots are very useful little stitches indeed when added to cross stitch. I use them to give extra definition to designs, for example on the rose border in the Garden Sampler on page 62. In many cases the stitch is added after the cross stitch is finished and worked in random patterns. Bring the needle up to the right side of the fabric, wind the thread around the needle twice and 'post' the needle through to the back, one thread or part of a block away

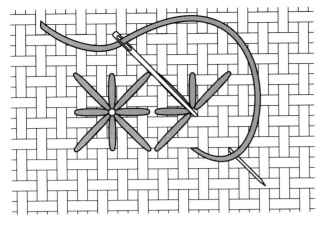

Algerian Eye

applied to cross stitch in the same way. If an area is defined, it is quite simple to select the shades that will work well together and then stitch at random.

Tweeding is a simple practice which multiplies the number of colours in your palate without buying more thread. To tweed, combine more than one coloured thread in the needle at the same time (see the Fruit and Vegetable Clock on page 38) and work as one. Where I have used this in the charts, you will see two numbers next to the colour in the key. When working French knots you can apply the tweeding in the same way (see the brambles in the Four Seasons Clock on page 13 and opposite).

PLANNING YOUR OWN DESIGNS

This section is included to help make the task of planning chart layouts much easier. It is also necessary because it is not possible to include complete charts for some of the larger designs in this book.

I always use Chartwell graph paper with a light-grey grid and a light, but not white, background. I usually use the imperial version, ie 10 squares per inch (2.5cm), which makes counting squares easier.

It is not necessary to copy all the detail when planning layouts. The coloured charts in this book are drawn with a solid outline, which you may choose not to stitch, but can be copied simply to mark the position of motifs within the overall design.

Decide on the completed size of the stitched project and choose which fabric you intend to use. You should at least have selected the thread count, if not the actual fabric.

Mark on the graph paper with a soft pencil where the centre and the extremes of the chart should appear. This becomes the master sheet.

Using a soft pencil, copy the outlines of the motifs you have selected on to another piece of graph paper. If only one half of a symmetrical design is illustrated, copy out one side and reverse it using the window method, as follows. Choose a large pane of glass and carefully tape the drawing to the glass with the back facing you. You will see that the design can be reversed and turned upside-down and then traced on to your master sheet.

When you have copied all the motifs you require it is quite simple to cut out each section and lay it in position on the master sheet. When you are satisfied with the layout

you can begin stitching, using the colour charts from the book.

PLANNING CLOCK FACES AND HEIGHT CHARTS

If you are intending to use a clock face in your design, select a purchased clock first before you plan your layouts. Mark the position of the hand spindle on the graph paper with a soft pencil. Looking at the chart, place the numerals 12 and 6 at the top and bottom of the face, followed by the 9 and 3 at either side. It is then quite simple to add the remaining numerals by sight.

Position of clock numerals

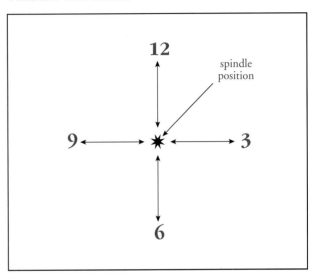

WASHING AND PRESSING CROSS STITCH

When a piece of cross stitch is complete, it may be necessary to wash the item before finishing. Washing can give a piece of stitching a new lease of life, but it can also ruin your work if care is not taken. Drinks, ice cream and cats can also cause real disasters, so always keep your stitching covered and well away from all of them!

If it does become necessary to wash a piece of stitching, DMC or Anchor threads are usually colour-fast, though some bright reds can bleed, so always check for colour-fastness before immersing the project completely. To do this, dampen a white tissue and press the red stitches at the back of the work. Remove the tissue and check for any traces of red colour. If any colour is visible on the tissue, avoid washing this project.

If the item is colour-fast, wash it in warm water by hand using bleach-free soap, squeezing gently but never rubbing or wringing. Rinse with plenty of clean water and lay the item in a clean towel. Squeeze the towel to remove most of the excess water, then allow the material to dry naturally. Do not use a tumble drier.

To iron cross stitch, heat the iron to a hot setting and use the steam button, if your iron has one. Cover the ironing board with a *thick* layer of towelling. I use four layers of bath towels. Place the stitching on the towelling, right side down, with the back of the work facing you. Press the fabric

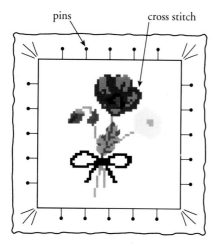

pins   cross stitch

Placing pins around project to stitch

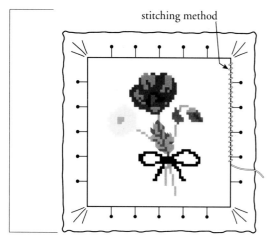

stitching method

Stitching method

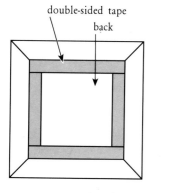

double-sided tape
back

folded excess material
lacing

Taping method   Lacing method

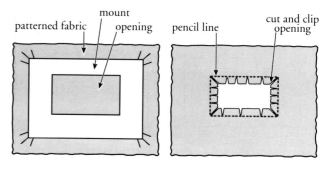

patterned fabric   mount   opening   pencil line   cut and clip opening

Covered mounts – stages 1 and 2

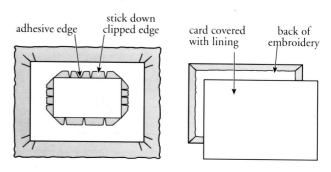

adhesive edge   stick down clipped edge   card covered with lining   back of embroidery

Covered mounts – stages 3 and 4

board, or you could possibly cover a piece of board with cotton fixed with a rubber-based adhesive and left to dry.

There are three methods of attaching the needlework to the board before framing:

● Pin the work to the edge of the board and stick in place with double-sided tape.

● Pin to a covered board and stitch in position.

● Pin to the board and lace across the back with strong linen thread.

When you pin the material to the board, it must be centred and stretched evenly, because any wobbles will show when the design is framed. Measure the board across the bottom edge and mark the centre with a pin. Match this to the centre of the bottom edge of the embroidery and, working outwards from the centre, pin through the fabric, following a line of threads until all four sides are pinned (see diagram). Either stitch through the needlework to the covered board, fix with double-sided tape or lace the excess fabric across the back.

COVERED MOUNTS

The most simple piece of needlework will be given extra depth by adding a covered stitched mount to co-ordinate with the design. If you intend to use an oval or circular-shaped mount, you will certainly need to buy it, as to cut these yourself is almost impossible. Square or rectangular mounts can be cut using a craft knife, as the rough edges will be covered by the material. Press the embroidery on the wrong side and stretch and mount as described previously. Cut the mount card the same size as the mounted embroidery and cut a window opening to the size you require. If the mount has been purchased, check the opening is large enough for the embroidery and set aside.

Using the mount as a template, cut a piece of fabric or the cross stitch project at least 1inch (2.5cm) wider all the way round. Place the fabric right side down on a clean flat

quite firmly and you will see how much this improves the appearance of your stitching. Leave the embroidery to cool and dry completely before framing or making up as desired.

STRETCHING AND MOUNTING

When mounting small cards or novelty projects, the whole procedure cam be completed using double-sided sticky tape, but it is worth taking more time and effort on larger projects. You will need acid-free mounting board, or a lightweight foam

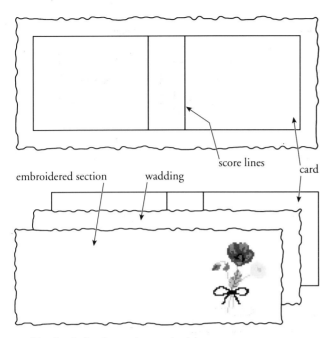

embroidered section   wadding

score lines   card

Making books by the scoring method

surface and draw around the inside of the opening with a soft pencil. Remove the mount and, using a sharp pair of pointed scissors, cut out the opening about ½inch (1.25cm) from the pencil line. Clip the edge at intervals.

On the wrong side of the mount, apply a thin layer of adhesive to the edge of the opening and add the fabric, checking the design is in the right position. Stick down and leave to dry. Complete the procedure by pinning and securing the excess material as described before.

MAKING BOOKS

To make up books or folders, one of two methods can be used. The scoring method enables the book or folder to be made up in one piece (see diagram). The stitching method involves making the book or folder in individual sections and then joining them together. In both cases, a softer look can be achieved by covering the card with polyester wadding before making up. If you intend to use the scoring method you must ensure that the original piece of fabric is large enough to wrap around the card in one section. When the stitching is complete, press on the wrong side and set aside.

Making books by the stitching method

inside front   spine

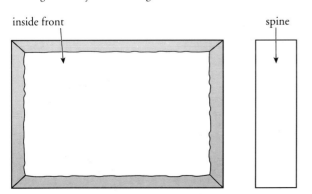

If you decide to use the scoring method you will need a piece of stiff card – mount card is ideal. It should be large enough to make the front, back and spine of the book. Lay the card on a clean, flat surface and, using a sharp craft knife, score as illustrated in the diagram and fold the card, thus forming the spine. Lay the card on a flat surface and cover with a piece of wadding slightly larger than the card. Sandwich this to the card with the embroidery, checking the position of the stitching. Using the pinning method described previously pin in position. Trim the excess fabric away, leaving 1inch (2.5cm) around the edge and secure this with strips of double-sided sticky tape. Pressing gently on the scored areas as you do it, fold the front and back up to check that the fabric is secure and then set aside whilst the lining is prepared. Cut a piece of co-ordinating fabric for the lining at least 1inch (2.5 cm) larger than the completed book and fold the raw edges inside. Slip stitch in position (see diagram).

For the stitching method, you will need three pieces of card: the front, the back and the spine. To cover them you will need the embroidery, a matching piece of fabric for the back and a strip for the spine. Cut a piece of lining fabric and wadding to match each section. The idea is that you make three 'sandwiches' (see diagram) from the lining, card, polyester wadding and the embroidery or back section. To make up one section proceed as follows. Lay the lining right side down on a flat surface, then lay the card on top. Add the wadding and finally the embroidery right side up. Folding in the raw edges, slip stitch invisibly all the way round. Complete all three sections in the same way and finally stitch all three pieces together using matching threads.

MAKING CARDS

If you wish to make cards, you should first refer to the section on planning your own designs and calculate the design size before selecting motifs for a particular card. When the

fold this section in   adhesive   opening

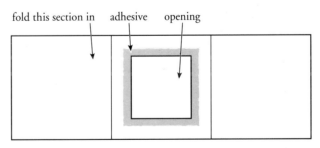

Making up a card

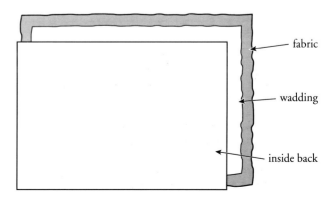

fabric

wadding

inside back

cross stitch is complete, press on the wrong side and make up in the following way. Unfold the card and position the cross stitch correctly, trimming away any excess fabric. Open out the card and cover the back face of the opening with a thin coat of adhesive. Stick down the fabric and the third fold of the card. Make sure that no adhesive oozes out and place the completed design aside to dry. Double-sided sticky tape can be used instead of glue, if preferred.

FRAMING

As I am sure you will have seen from the wonderful colour photographs in the earlier sections of the book, the way a design is framed can greatly affect the end appearance. Framing by a professional can be very expensive, particularly if you want something a little different, but all the framing and finishing techniques suggested in this book can be tackled successfully by the amateur at home, and this will save a lot of money.

When choosing a frame for a finished project, select the largest moulding you can afford and don't worry if the colour is unsuitable. The magic ingredient is car spray paint. Experiment until you find a shade which suits, as I did with the frames in this book. Coloured polishes, liming wax, acrylic paints and matt varnish can also create super effects, and I have added a single gold slip to each frame after painting or waxing.

MAKING UP

DRAWSTRING BAGS

A drawstring bag is a very simple but effective way of completing a cross stitch project. The Odd Sock Sack on pages 48-9 is a good example of this and could be adapted easily to make school shoe bags and sacks for sports kit.

Two pieces of patterned background fabric
Stitched linen band
Matching sewing thread
Two lengths of ecru-coloured string

1 When the cross stitch is complete, press the stitching on the wrong side (see Washing and Pressing Cross Stitch on pages 127-8).
2 Cut two pieces of background fabric at least 5inches (13cm) larger than the completed size. Place one piece right side

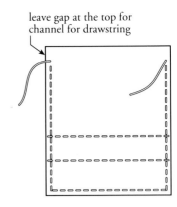

leave gap at the top for channel for drawstring

Leave sides open for drawstring

up on a clean flat surface. Position the stitched linen band across the width of the material. Check the photograph on pages 48-9 if you are not sure where. Pin in place. Using a sewing machine or small back stitches, stitch the band to the background fabric using matching thread. Press lightly on the wrong side.
3 To complete the bag, use the two pieces of background fabric and pin right sides together matching raw edges. Machine or hand stitch around three sides through all thicknesses (see diagram) allowing a 1inch (2.5cm) seam allowance. Neaten or oversew the raw edges and press seams open.
4 Fold in the top section and machine or hand stitch two lines across the width of the bag, leaving a small gap at each side seam (see diagram).
5 Thread a piece of string or ribbon through this channel along the front and back section leaving at least 5inches (13cm) of string at each end. Pull the drawstring gently and tie with a figure of eight knot at each end.

PLAIN BAG WITH HANDLE

A lined bag with a strong handle can be used for shopping, school kit, or, as illustrated on pages 100-1, the Gone Fishing Picnic Bag.

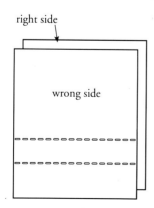

right side

wrong side

Stitching around three sides of bag

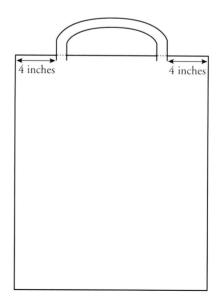

4 inches   4 inches

Position marked for handles

Two bag sections, one with stitched design
Extra fabric to make handles
Lining fabric or calico
Matching sewing thread

1 Make up as for the drawstring bag, stitching the three sides together as above.
2 Cut two pieces of lining fabric the same size as the bag sections. Stitch three sides together as above, neaten the raw edges and press seams open. Turn the stitched design to the right side, pressing seams open. Insert the lining section into the bag, wrong sides together matching side seams and pin in position. Fold the raw edges inside along the top edge and pin.
3 Make two handles as follows. Cut two strips of matching fabric at least 4inches (10cm) wide and 18inches (46cm) long. Fold these sections in half along the length, folding in the raw edges. Pin in position. Machine or hand stitch along the edge with matching thread.
4 Press with a steam iron.
5 Measure across the top of the bag, marking a point 4inches (10cm) from both side seams. Place one end of the handle between the bag and lining section and pin in position. Repeat this until two handles are formed (see diagram). Using a sewing machine or small back stitches, stitch along the top edge of the bag through all thicknesses with matching thread.

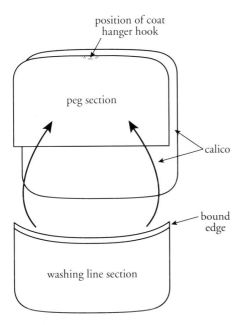

How to combine peg bag sections

WASH-DAY PEG BAG

To complete the pretty bag as illustrated on page 48, you will need to make or purchase bias binding to match the design.
1 Cut a piece of calico lining fabric the size and shape of your peg bag, remembering to check the size of the coat hanger you are intending to use.
2 Shape the four corners of the lining so they are rounded. Shape the matching corners of the stitched sections in the same way (see diagram). Work a narrow hem along the bottom edge of the stitched peg section to prevent fraying.

Press hem. Lay the calico lining on a clean flat surface, lay the peg section on top, matching the top raw edges (see diagram). Mark the position of the coat hanger hook with a tacking (basting) stitch.
3 Bind the top edge of the stitched washing line section with bias binding (see Bias Binding on page). Press lightly and lay the washing line section on top of the lining and peg sections (see diagram), matching the bottom raw edges. Pin and tack (baste) in position. Add the bias binding all the way round, using a sewing machine or with small back stitches, leaving a small opening for the coat hanger hook. Top stitch the binding from the right side, carefully following the edge with the machine needle and leaving a gap for the hook.
4 Cover the hook with matching fabric, slip the coat hanger inside the stitched sections and up through the gap. To finish, add a fabric bow.

HEIGHT CHART

Use this section to complete the Air Balloon Height Chart.

A pair of bell-pull ends
Completed cross stitch
Pelmet Vilene
Cotton thread
Lining fabric

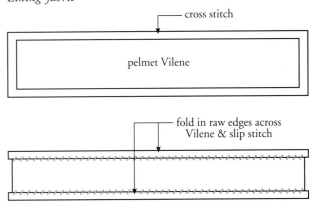

Folding raw edges across pelmet lining

1 When the cross stitch is complete, press on the wrong side and lay on a clean flat surface, right side down.
2 Cut a piece of pelmet lining to the completed dimensions and lay on top of the stitched section. Carefully fold the long edge over the Vilene and trim the excess material to ⅝inch (2cm). Catch the edge down with matching thread, taking care not to stitch through to the right side.
3 Completing the top section first, make a fold 2inches (5cm) from the top and slip a bell-pull end in position. Catch the raw edge down, again taking care not to stitch through to the right side. Repeat this operation at the bottom.
4 Cut a piece of lining and, folding in a narrow hem, pin to the back of the chart. Slip stitch the lining to the back of the design, using matching thread.

ANEMONE STOCKING SACHET

1 Using sharp scissors, round the corners of the stitched section slightly (see the colour photograph on page 109).
2 Cut a piece of lining material and polyester wadding using the stitched piece of linen as a pattern.

3 Lay the stitched piece face down on a clean flat surface (stitching at the top), cover with a piece of wadding and then lining fabric. Pin and tack round the edges through all the layers. Trim away any excess.

4 Using bias binding and the method described overleaf, bind the short edge, nearest to you. Make a fold a third of the way along and fold up the bound edge to make a pocket. Match the raw edges, pin and tack in position.

5 To join the pocket sides, bind the edges together with bias binding, starting at the fold, continuing around the curved section and finishing at the other side of the fold.

6 To add the lace flounce, cut a piece of lace three times the width of the case. Gather loosely to fit the curved edge. Slip lace under binding prior to final row of stitching, and machine stitch through the binding, lace and fabric. Finish off any ends and shake the lace out to fall naturally, without pressing.

WILD ROSE JEWELLERY ROLL

The inside of the jewellery roll (page 109) includes one large pocket, two small pockets and a simple sausage shape on which to keep rings.

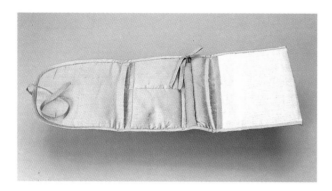

Inside of the jewellery roll

1 Using sharp scissors, shape the two corners of the stitched section (see photograph).

2 Press the stitched linen on the wrong side and cut pieces of lining fabric and polyester wadding to the same size and shape as the linen.

3 Cut another piece of lining fabric, 9 x 3½inches (23 x 9cm), which will become the pockets in the lining. Fold in both long edges of this piece and hem one of them invisibly. Pin in position to the right side of the lining, at one end, as shown. Machine stitch to the lining along the folded

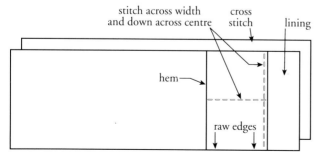

Placing the pocket in lining

unhemmed edge and up the centre to form two small pockets.

4 Lay the linen right side down on a clean flat surface and cover with the wadding. Cover with the lining, right side up, with the small pockets over the cross stitched end of the linen. Pin and tack the raw edges together through all layers.

5 Bind the short straight edge with bias binding (see overleaf). Fold the bound edge up, folding along the first line of tacking in the linen, to form the main pocket. Pin and tack the sides of the pocket together and join them by binding with bias binding, starting from one side of the fold, continuing round the curved section and finishing at the other side of the fold. Make two ties from ribbon or bias binding and attach to fasten when the jewellery roll is folded as shown in the photograph.

6 The optional ring holder is a tube made from the lining fabric, stuffed with wadding and attached with press studs.

FOOTSTOOLS AND PADDED SEATS

The basic principles for making any padded projects are very similar. Pin cushions, footstools and seats are made exactly the same way, in different scales.

1 For the footstool shown in the picture on page 24, complete the cross stitch and press on the wrong side.

2 Remove the screws from the underneath of the footstool and remove the pad.

3 Lay the stitched fabric on top of the pad, check the position and carefully pin around the edge as illustrated, pulling firmly and gradually removing any creases or folds. When you are happy with the appearance of the stitching, trim away any excess fabric and lace the remainder under the base.

4 When complete, place back in the wooden surround and replace the screws.

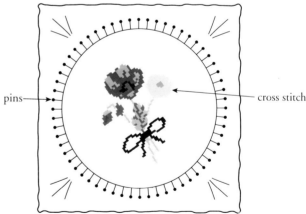

Placing pins around the edge of the footstool

APRONS

1 To make the apron, make a paper pattern as illustrated, and cut out your fabric.

2 Bind round the edges of the apron with suitable bias binding (see overleaf), adding ties for the neck and waist as you stitch.

3 If you are adding the pocket, bind the edges of the pocket with bias binding, then top stitch the pocket to the front of the apron.

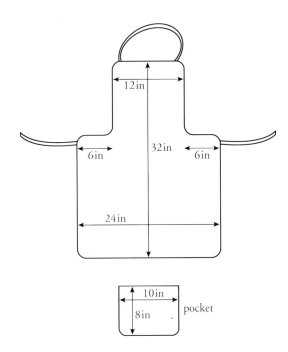

BIAS BINDING

Many of the projects in this book are completed using bias binding, which can be either purchased or home-made. To attach bias binding simply and quickly, by hand or with a sewing machine, proceed as follows.

1 Cut the binding to the correct length. Pin and stitch the binding to the wrong side of the project first, matching raw edges.

2 Fold the binding to the right side and top stitch in position. Press lightly.

MAKING TWISTED CORDS

Use this technique to make a simple cord for the Fisherman's Log Book on page 100-1.

1 Choose a colour or group of colours in stranded cottons (floss) to match the stitching. Cut a minimum of four lengths, four times the length of finished cord required.

2 Fold in half. Ask a friend to hold the two ends, whilst you slip a pencil through the loop at the other end. Twist the pencil and continue twisting until kinks appear. Walk slowly towards your partner and the cord will automatically twist.

3 Smooth out kinks from the looped end and tie a knot at the other end to secure.

SUPPLIERS

SPECIALIST LINENS, TOWELS AND AFGHANS

Spinning Jenny, Bradley, Keighley, West Yorkshire, BD20 9DD, UK. Tel: 0535 632469

Campden Needlecraft Centre, Chipping Campden, Glos, GL55 6AG, UK. Tel: 0386 840583

Wichelt Imports, Rural Route 1, Stoddard, W I 54658, USA. Tel: 608-788-4600

Stadia Handcrafts, PO Box 495, 85 Elizabeth Street, Paddington, NSW 2021, Australia. Tel: 02328 7973

LIBERTY FABRICS

Liberty plc, 210-220 Regent Street, London, W1R 6AH, UK. Tel: 071 734 1234

Liberty of London Inc, 108, West 39th Street, New York, NY10018, USA. Tel: 212 459 0080

Norman Vivian Pty Ltd, 18, Belmore Street, Surry Hills, NSW 2010, Australia. Tel: 2 212 1633

THREADS AND FABRICS

DMC Creative World Ltd, Pullman Road, Wigston, Leicestershire, LE18 2DY, UK. Tel: 0533 811040

DMC Corporation, Port Kearny, Building 10, South Kearny, New Jersey 07032, USA. Tel: 201 589 0606

DMC Needlecraft Pty Ltd, PO 317, Earlswood, NSW, Australia. Tel: 612 5593 088

THE INGLESTONE COLLECTION

The Inglestone Collection produces Jane Greenoff's counted cross stitch kits and charts, including some of the designs in this and previous books. These are available from most good needlework shops or, in case of difficulty, by mail order.

The Inglestone Collection also imports and distributes some of the more unusual products used by Jane Greenoff in *55 Country Cross Stitch Charts*, *Victorian Cross Stitch* and this book. Feel free to contact us if you have any difficulty finding a product, and we will direct you to a local source of supply.

Charts and complete kits are available for the following

designs in this book: The Garden Sampler, The Music Sampler, Flying, Boating, No Place Like Home and The Seaside Sampler. Ask at your local needlework shop for details, or write (enclosing an SAE) to Jane Greenoff, The Inglestone Collection, Yells Yard, Cirencester Road, Fairford, Glos GL7 4BS, UK, or telephone (0285) 712778.

In the USA, Jane Greenoff's books and kits are available from Designing Women Unlimited, 601, East Eighth Street, El Dorado, Arkansas 71730 USA, telephone 501-862-0021.

ACKNOWLEDGEMENTS

My grateful thanks to friends, neighbours and suppliers for their generous help and support during the preparation of this book.

To my husband Bill and my children James and Louise, who have allowed me to shut myself away for hours at a time with only a few interruptions.

To my special friend, Michel Standley, who organises The Inglestone Collection and keeps production running smoothly in spite of everything.

To Jean, Daphne, Liz, Diane and Betty, without whom everything would grind to a halt.

A special thank you to all my stitchers, who not only cross stitch day and night but contribute their ideas, comments and time to perfecting these charts and designs. They are Dorothy Presley, Hanne Castelo, Carol Lebez, Su Maddocks, Margaret Cornish, Sarah Haines, Sharon Griffiths, Sophie Bartlett, Kathy Elliot, Sarah Day, Jill Vaughan, Sam Sutton, Elizabeth Lydan and Vera Greenoff.

To Vivienne Wells at David & Charles for her continuous support and friendship and Di Lewis who has such wonderful ideas on both sides of the camera lens.

To Ethan Danielson for his quiet patience and the beautiful charts.

To Sarah Jane Gillespie of Yew Tree House, Symonds Yat West, Herefordshire for my beautiful line drawings.

To everyone at Oakland Builders for the things they do with wood.

To Jean and Frank Dittrich for hospitality and friendship.

To Linda Rogers for doughcraft trug.

To Sarah Shaw, who has supported my efforts since my daughter was born. Sue Rishton for finishing some of my special projects, and Susan Hawkins for her excellent cushion finishing service (contact Needleworks, The Old School House, Hall Road, Leckhampton, Cheltenham).

My parents, Pat and Eric Fowler, for the photograph of my grandparents and understanding why I don't write.

Beryl Lee at Artisan, High Street, Pinner, Middlesex for threads, fabrics and friendship.

To David and Jan Cohen, Burford Needlecraft, Burford, Oxon, for fishing tips and thread and fabric supplies.

To Clare for painting my lovely chair. To all at I L Soft for rescuing me when my printer died. To my dentist Peter Duff who drilled my shells. Robert Morgan for the long loan of his beautiful trumpet, and Ken and Ginnie Thompson for remembering me.

Sue and Margy at Designing Women for all their ideas, Joyce Wichelt for the very generous supplies of fabrics, and to all at Lamont, Northern Ireland, for their even-weave linens.

To Karl at Tunley and Son, Fleet Street, Swindon for my lovely frames, and all at Leverton Framing, Hungerford for the loan of frames and mounts.

Amanda Hutchinson at Liberty for all her advice and support over the last few years, and all at Below Stairs, Hungerford, Berks for the loan of lovely props.

Jean and Harry Wardlaw, The Sewing Basket, 4 Edinburgh Road, Formby, Liverpool for cards, frames and self-adhesive mount board. All at Jar Frames, 2 Beacon Close, Groby, Leicester for the games box, key cupboard and footstool.

To Mike Grey at Framecraft Miniatures Ltd.

INDEX